THE COMPLETE BOOK OF
Candlewick Embroidery

THE COMPLETE BOOK OF

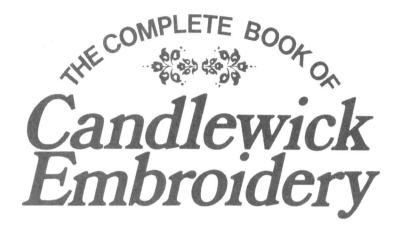

Candlewick Embroidery

·····❧ SUE MILLARD ❧·····

NEW
HOLLAND

First published in the UK in 1989 by New Holland (Publishers) Ltd
37 Connaught Street, London W2 2AZ

Reprinted 1991, 1992 and 1994

ISBN 1 85368 150 4 (pbk)

Editor: Linda de Villiers
Layout: Lellyn Creamer
Cover design: Etienne van Duyker
Photography: Alain Proust
Illustrations: Anneke Lipsanen
Line drawings: Sue Thompson

Typeset and reproduced by Sparhams (Pty) Ltd
Printed and bound in Singapore by Kyodo Printing Co.

PUBLISHER'S NOTE Imperial measurements have been adjusted or rounded up or down as
appropriate to help the reader.

CONTENTS

THE BASICS

Candlewicking is a most fascinating and beautiful form of embroidery that is easy to learn and quick to master. The basic stitches comprise French and colonial knots with finer details embroidered in satin stitch, stem stitch and back stitch. Candlewick embroidery is closely associated with quilting so this technique has also been fully explained.

Throughout the book I have given very detailed step-by-step instructions for each project. Please read through them carefully as the extra time spent in understanding each step will be well worth the effort. Prepare the fabric and cotton lace according to the directions given to prevent any subsequent shrinkage. Remember that accuracy at each stage is very important as it will save you a great deal of time when assembling each item.

I have included projects for both the beginner and the experienced needlewoman, but none is really difficult to do – some just take longer than others. All the items are completely washable and, therefore, practical and pleasurable to use.

An added advantage of calico is that it tones in with all colour schemes so that you can move the candlewicked accessories from one room to another and never grow tired of looking at them.

Whatever projects you decide to make, I hope they give you as much joy and happiness as they have given me. I trust that this book will inspire you to make lovely accessories for your own home as well as beautiful gifts you will be proud to give away.

MATERIALS

FABRIC

Originally traditional candlewick embroidery was done on unshrunk 100 per cent cotton calico or muslin. Once the embroidery was complete the fabric was washed in very hot water to shrink the fabric and hold the embroidery stitches firmly in place. Each damp square was then stretched on a blocking board until quite dry before being made into the chosen article. The fabric was never ironed, giving the candlewicked fabric that traditional puckered look.

Today we have lovely fabrics on the market including very good quality 100 per cent cotton calico that is available both preshrunk and unshrunk. Although the unshrunk fabric is usually very stiff, it does wash very well.

NOTE Many people use a polyester and cotton blend curtain lining, but as it often shrinks it should be prepared in the same way as unshrunk cotton calico. With this particular fabric, the warp thread is made from cotton while the weft thread is made from polyester; it is the cotton that shrinks.

PREPARATION OF FABRIC

UNSHRUNK CALICO Place the entire piece of fabric in a bath of *plain, cold water* overnight. Hot water will 'cook' the starch into the fabric. You will then not be able to remove the starch and as a result the fabric will not be nearly as soft. It is important not to add any washing powder or fabric softener. (The fabric lying below the surface of the water will be bleached by the washing powder, whereas the fabric lying above the water line because of the air pockets that form, will not be bleached.)

The following day wash the fabric in the washing machine on the hot cycle, using washing powder and fabric softener. Press while still damp.

PRESHRUNK CALICO Wash in the washing machine on a hot washing cycle, using washing powder and fabric softener. Press while still damp.

COTTON LACE

Cotton lace, however good the quality, always shrinks a little.

PREPARATION OF LACE

Wash all cotton lace in very hot water or boil it in plain water for 15-20 minutes. Place the lace in a towel and wring dry.

Iron one end of the lace dry, then measure the width. On an old piece of fabric, draw two parallel lines the width you have measured, to make a template. Iron the lace lengthways, using the template as a guide to ensure an even width throughout.

THE HOOP

It is essential to use a hoop for candlewick embroidery. Buy a 30 cm (12 in) or 35 cm (14 in) quilting hoop as this can be used for embroidery as well as for quilting. Having the hoop mounted on a base will leave both hands free to do the embroidery.

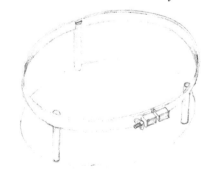

THE NEEDLES

You will need a sharp, large-eyed, sturdy needle such as a No. 22 Chenille needle or a No. 7 crewel embroidery needle. A tapestry needle is unsuitable as it tends to snag the fabric.

TO THREAD A NEEDLE Once a length of thread is cut, it tends to unravel rapidly and there is nothing more frustrating than trying to thread a needle with a badly unravelled thread. To avoid this happening, only cut the thread once the needle has been threaded. Hold the loose end of the thread in your left hand between your thumb and forefinger. Place the needle in your right hand and press the eye of the needle over the loose end of the thread. Now cut the thread.

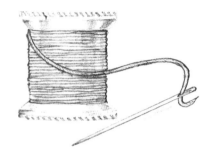

TO MAKE A KNOT Hold the loose end of the thread and the threaded needle between your left thumb and forefinger as shown. Now wrap the thread round the needle once and pull the needle through the loop. A good secure knot will be formed.

THE THREAD

Although specially manufactured candlewicking thread is not always available, there are many suitable substitutes available. Various types of 100 per cent mercerized cotton and embroidery floss are most suitable and any of the embroidery stitches worked in these threads look beautiful. I prefer a matt, four-ply 100 per cent knitting cotton to work the knots, but try experimenting with a combination of shiny and matt cottons to give an interesting texture to the finished article.

NOTE Before using coloured thread, test it for colour-fastness by washing it in very hot water.

Cut an old piece of calico or any plain fabric about 40 cm (16 in) square, place it securely in the hoop and pull it taut. First practise doing the three different knots (French, bullion and colonial) in single threads of different types. Then try using a double thread; that is, thread a single thread approximately 80 cm (32 in) long through the eye of the needle. Bring the ends together and form a knot.

I suggest you experiment with different threads. Try using two or three strands of silky embroidery floss combined with a matt knitting cotton, or perhaps two or three different shades of embroidery floss together. These two combinations of threads add great interest and depth to your work. I often use two or three different types of thread to candlewick the designs for a quilt, using the thicker matt knitting cotton double to accentuate the most important sections of the design.

For the more delicate embroidery stitches, it is best to use No. 5, No. 8 or any cotton thread of a similar thickness. Although it is not traditional, I have, on occasion, also used a No. 5 acrylic crochet thread. It washes extremely well and looks very pretty. On the other hand, you might like to candlewick your quilt traditionally, using only one type of matt thread throughout.

Check the tension of your work to ensure that the knots are lying flat and secure on the fabric. The knots must not be floppy or loose as this will make the work look untidy.

By practising beforehand you will be able to ascertain which type and thickness of thread best suits you.

TRACING MEDIUM

Use a water-soluble marking pen. This is the only pen that works really efficiently as the ink only remains on the fabric until the square is washed. Marks made by other felt-tip or ballpoint pens are impossible to remove.

TRACING THE DESIGN ONTO THE FABRIC

NOTE Before tracing the design, it is very important to find the centre of the fabric and the design in order to position the design accurately on the fabric.

To find the centre of a square of fabric, fold it in half vertically and then in half horizontally. Draw your thumbnail across the folds to make a crease. Measure the design at its widest point from the extreme left to the extreme right. Draw a vertical line at the halfway mark. Turn the design round and do the same top-to-bottom. The point where the lines cross is your centre point.

Place the centre point of the fabric square over the centre point of the design and pin them together.

If the design is dark enough you will be able to see it right through the fabric. Trace the design onto the fabric in a solid line as shown in the designs at the back of the book.

NOTE You may come across designs where the dots are unevenly spaced. This inaccuracy is clearly visible once the embroidery is complete. If the dots on the design you are using are inaccurately spaced, use dressmaker's carbon and a tracing wheel to trace the design onto the fabric, then work the knots (French, bullion and colonial) on every second mark made by the tracing wheel. However, this does depend on the thickness of the thread; with very fine thread you would work a knot on each dot.

Another method is to stick the design and fabric square onto a windowpane with masking tape before tracing the design.

A third method is to rest a piece of glass on top of two blocks (one block beneath either side of the glass) and to place a torch or bedside light underneath the glass. Place the design and then the fabric square on top of the glass and trace the design onto the fabric. The design shows up very clearly with the light shining beneath it. (A glass-topped coffee table works very well.) If you intend doing a great deal of candlewicking, it would be a good idea to invest in a piece of perspex as it is unbreakable.

TO ENLARGE OR REDUCE A DESIGN

The easiest way to enlarge or reduce a design is on a photocopying machine but for those who don't have access to one, it is preferable to use the grid method. Make an evenly squared grid over the design, then draw another grid the size you would like the design to be. This second grid must have the same number of squares as the first. Now draw the design square by square.

original design

enlarged design

STITCHES

Antique candlewick quilts seen in American museums reveal that the stitches used most frequently by early American candlewickers were large French knots, satin stitch and back stitch. Several other stitches were added later, for example colonial knots, chain stitch and stem stitch.

Today many different stitches can be incorporated most successfully into your designs.

FRENCH KNOT Working from left to right, bring the needle through from the back to the front of the fabric. *Hold the thread towards you* between the left thumb and forefinger. Hold the needle between the right thumb and forefinger. Wrap the thread around the needle once and insert it just to the right of where the thread first emerged. Let the loop formed rest over your left forefinger or thumb and move your finger or thumb about to adjust the shape of the knot. Slip the loop off your finger at the last moment. Pull the needle and thread through to the back until the knot rests quite firmly on the fabric, then come up through the fabric again to execute the next knot. The thread may be used double to produce larger knots. To finish off, run the needle under several stitches at the back of the work.

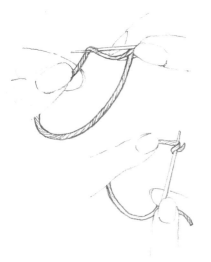

When the thread is wrapped around the needle twice, the stitch is called a bullion knot and shouldn't be confused with the bullion stitch.

SATIN STITCH Satin stitches are straight stitches worked close together, evenly and neatly. Begin across the centre and work towards the end of the design. Turn the work around and complete the other half. Try not to overlap any of the stitches. To finish off, run the needle through the stitches at the back of the work.

BACK STITCH Working from right to left, bring the needle up at A. Go down at B and come back up at C. Go down at A and come up at D. Continue in this manner making all the stitches equal in length. To finish off, run the needle under several stitches at the back of the work.

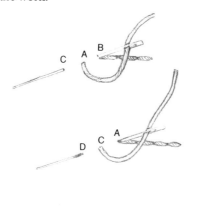

EXTRA EMBROIDERY STITCHES

BULLION STITCH is best worked on fabric which is stretched in a hoop, thus leaving both hands free to work the stitch. Bring the thread to the front at B and insert the needle a short distance away at A. Allow the needle to re-emerge at B. Do not pull the needle through completely. Wrap the thread round the needle six or seven times, gently place the left thumb on the coil and pull the needle through carefully. Insert the needle at A to secure the stitch.

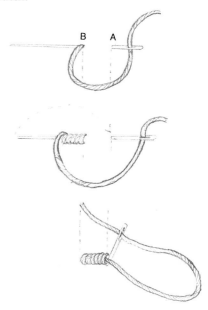

STEM STITCH Stem stitch is worked from left to right. Come up at A. Hold the thread below the stitching line, go down at B and come up at C. Go down at D and come up at E.

Continue in this manner, keeping the stitches equal in length. On a sharp curve, make your stitches smaller to accommodate the curve.

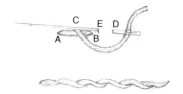

CHAIN STITCH is ideal to use on heavy outlines. Working from right to left, bring the needle up through the surface of the fabric at A. Form a loop with the thread and re-insert the needle at A, coming up at B inside the loop. Pull the thread through, keeping the looped thread below the point of the needle. Re-insert the needle at B leaving a loop. Come up at C which is inside the loop and pull the thread through as before, keeping the looped thread below the point of the needle.

To finish off, secure the last loop by bringing the thread over the loop and pulling the needle through to the back of the work. Run the needle under several stitches.

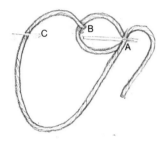

CORAL STITCH is worked from right to left. Bring the thread through the fabric at A, lay the thread along the line of the design and hold it down with your left thumb. Make a small stitch (through the fabric) underneath the line and thread. Keeping the circle of thread below the point of the needle, pull the thread through to form a small knot. I use this stitch to embroider butterflies' feelers and the stamens of flowers.

FISHBONE STITCH is used to embroider leaves and the bodies of butterflies. Work from top to bottom along the centre line of the design. Bring the thread through at A. Insert the needle at B. Pull the needle and thread through at C. Re-insert the needle just below B and pull the needle and thread through at D. Continue working from the centre to the right and then from the centre to the left until you have completed the design. Work the stitches evenly and close together so that no ground fabric is visible.

To finish off, run the needle under several stitches at the back of the work.

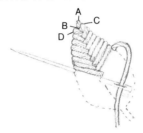

COLONIAL KNOT Working from left to right and holding the thread and needle as you would for a French knot, bring the thread to the front of the cloth at A. Push the needle under the thread, then take the thread over and under the point of the needle to form a figure eight. Re-insert the needle to the right of where the needle first emerged, pulling the needle and thread through to the back of the fabric and tightening the knot exactly the same way as you did for the French knot.

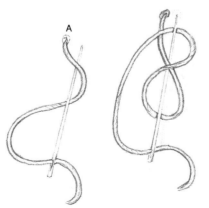

FEATHER STITCH This decorative and quick stitch is easy to perfect and makes an attractive feathery line, whether worked on straight lines or along curves. I often use this stitch to embroider hearts and the veins of leaves.

Working from top to bottom along a centre line, bring the thread up at A. Hold the thread down with the left thumb. On the right-hand side of the centre line, with the thread forming a circle to the right, make a small slanted stitch towards the centre line, keeping the thread below the needle point. Pull the needle and thread through. With the thread forming a circle to the left and on the left-hand side of the centre line, again hold the thread down with the thumb. Make a small slanted stitch towards the centre line, keeping the thread below the needle point. Pull the needle and thread through. Continue in this manner making small slanted stitches (towards the centre line) first to the right and then to the left.

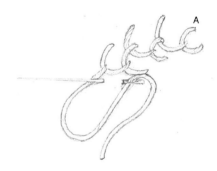

QUILTING

Quilting adds dimension and depth to any project, whether it is used on a candlewicked design or on the border of your quilt.

MATERIALS

A THIMBLE is absolutely essential if you want to prevent raw, punctured fingers. A thimble is used to push the needle through one or more layers of fabric. You will need to wear one on the middle finger of your right hand if you are right-handed (or the middle finger of your left hand if you are left-handed). It is also sensible to wear a rubber fingerguard (turned inside out) on the index or middle finger of your left hand.

NEEDLES used for quilting should be short, sharp and strong, preferably No. 9 or 10 'between' needles. Thread several needles at once, as very often a quilting design has several rows of stitching that need to be worked on simultaneously, and it will save you having to stop and re-thread a single needle too many times.

THREAD   Strong 100 per cent pure cotton quilting thread or specially waxed quilting thread is needed. If the thread has not already been waxed, run it through a piece of beeswax to make it easier to pull through the fabric. Use 40-45 cm (16-18 in) lengths and make a knot at one end.

A QUILTING HOOP with a diameter of 30-35 cm (12-14 in), preferably mounted on a base, makes the quilting of the squares much easier. Large free-standing quilting frames are available and are most useful for quilting very large projects. Unfortunately they take up rather a lot of space, so for the average quilter they are a little impractical. Many people quilt sections of a project, such as the borders of a quilt, with the work resting on a table or their lap.

WADDING/BATTING is available in various thicknesses; for instance 68-100 g wadding/batting is available in most countries. Be sure to use sheet wadding/batting and not polyester stuffing, which is only intended for stuffing pillows and so on. For most quilted projects a thin wadding/batting is the easiest and most suitable to use.

BACKING FABRIC   Use the same calico or fabric that you used for the front of the project. It is preferable not to use a cheaper grade of calico or fabric for the backing as the results may be disappointing.

PREPARING TO QUILT

To prepare for quilting, it is essential to tack the three layers (the backing, wadding/batting and the front) of the project together.
 Place the backing fabric, wrong side up, on the floor or a flat surface. Place the wadding/batting on top of this, making sure that you smooth out any creases in the backing or wadding/batting. Centre the quilt top (or whatever project you are doing) on top of the wadding/batting.
 Pin the three layers together, starting from the centre and working towards the centre point of the outside edges. Then pin from the centre to the corners.
 Tack along these rows of pins. Continue to tack until you have done at least 32 rows of tacking for a large project and at least eight for a small project such as a cushion. The quilting will be easier and neater the more you tack. The extra effort is definitely worthwhile.

QUILTING STITCHES

Two basic stitches are used for hand quilting. I use back stitch for quilting the designs on the candlewicked squares and short running stitches for quilting the borders.
 The secret of beautiful quilting is small, straight, evenly-spaced stitches

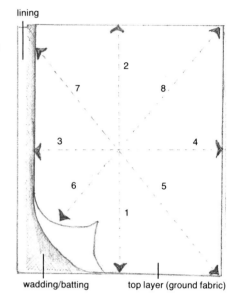

lining

wadding/batting   top layer (ground fabric)

worked as close together as you can. With practise you can achieve eight to twelve stitches per 2.5 cm (1 in).
 Longer stitches are perfectly acceptable but to look their best, they must be neatly and evenly spaced both back and front.

RUNNING STITCH   Thread the needle and make a knot at one end. Work a large stitch through the top fabric and wadding/batting and give a little tug so that the knot becomes buried in the wadding/batting. Come out at the starting point.

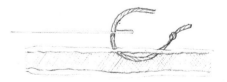

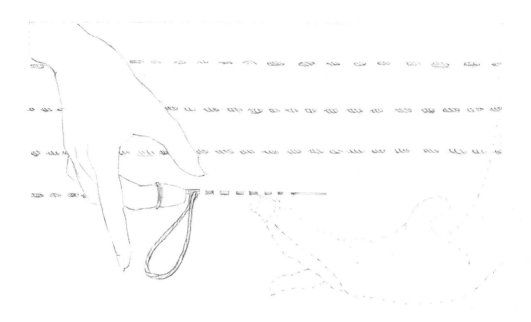

With the thimble on the middle finger of the right hand, push the needle vertically through all three layers until it touches the middle finger of the left hand (which you have placed underneath the project). Tilt the needle quickly so that it makes a small stitch at the back and continue to push the needle up through to the front again. Hold the work in place with the left thumb. Your right wrist must be quite relaxed as you will see that the movement is rather like that of a see-saw as the needle is pushed in and out of the fabric. Try to put several stitches on the needle before pulling it right through the fabric.

BACK STITCH I like to use this stitch when quilting the designs on all my candlewicked projects. I work a back stitch beneath each French or colonial knot so that the quilting stitches are not visible but the effect is still the same.

For this method of quilting you will need to place the fabric in a quilting hoop. Remove the outer hoop, place the project to be quilted straight down over the inner hoop, then replace and tighten the outer hoop. (The outer hoop should not be very tight and the fabric must have a little slack.) Turn the hoop upside down and check that there are no creases underneath. If there are, ease the creases away by pulling the fabric very gently. Now you are ready to quilt.

Make a knot at the end of the thread and push the needle and thread through the top fabric and wadding/batting, coming up again under a French or colonial knot. Give the thread a little tug so that the knot becomes buried in the wadding/batting (see opposite).

Place the left index or middle finger under the first French or colonial knot, pushing it up slightly. Insert the needle into the fabric just behind where the thread first emerged and push it vertically through all three layers until the needle touches the finger underneath. Tilt the needle quickly and push it diagonally through the wadding/batting, coming up under the next French or colonial knot. The quicker you tilt the needle, the smaller the stitch at the back will be. Continue in this manner, working a back stitch under each knot.

To end the row of quilting, tie a knot in the thread about 1 cm (½ in) from the fabric and do a back stitch coming up through the wadding/batting and top fabric a little distance away. Tug gently and the knot will disappear into the wadding/batting. Cut off the remaining thread.

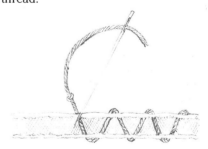

Once the whole project has been quilted, remove the tacking threads.

THE KITCHEN

So many hours are spent in the kitchen every day that it is worthwhile making it an attractive room in which to work. Autumn sunshine, gleaming copper and just-picked roses in this farmhouse kitchen set the scene for these pretty candlewick embroidered creations. Ruffled cottage curtains, apron and oven gloves are charming additions to any kitchen, while the white on white embroidered tray cloth and tea cosy add an air of elegance to this rustic setting.

Towels, a wall-hanging, tablecloth and lampshade are but a few of the other beautifully embroidered projects featured in this book that can be made for this very important room.

TEA COSY

Two different methods of making a tea cosy are described here: in the first method the tea cosy is quilted while in the second the cover is removable and, therefore, cannot be quilted.

Materials for quilted tea cosy
38 cm x 26 cm-wide (15 in x 10 ¼ in-wide) tracing paper
52 cm x 70 cm-wide (20 ½ in x 27 ½ in-wide) fabric
52 cm x 35 cm-wide (20 ½ in x 13 ¾ in-wide) medium-weight polyester wadding/batting
1.4 m x 3 cm-wide (1 ½ yds x 1 ¼ in) cotton lace or broderie anglaise for the frill

1. Fold the tracing paper in half vertically and trace the tea cosy pattern and design on page 76, completing the pattern and design by tracing first one half and then the other.

2. Fold the fabric in half horizontally so that it measures 26 cm x 70 cm (10 ¼ in x 27 ½ in) wide and press the fold firmly. This horizontal line will become the base line of the tea cosy. Open out the fabric and place it on top of the pattern,

matching the base line of the pattern with the fold of the fabric.

3. Trace the outline and designs onto the fabric. Trace off a second outline and designs alongside the first one. Do not cut out. (See fig 1.)

4. Place the fabric in a hoop, pull taut and candlewick all four designs.

5. Refold the fabric horizontally and cut out the two sections of the tea cosy along the traced outlines, but not along the fold.

6. Following the instructions on page 8, wash and iron both pieces of candlewicked fabric, then refold horizontally.

7. Fold the wadding/batting in half horizontally and trace the outline of the tea cosy pattern onto the wadding/batting. Cut out along the outlines, then along the fold line. You will now have two pieces of wadding/batting the shape of a tea cosy.

8. Sandwich one piece of wadding/batting between each of the folded tea cosy shapes. (See fig 2.)

9. Following the instructions on page 12, quilt each of the two sections separately. Quilt only those parts of the designs that you wish to accentuate.

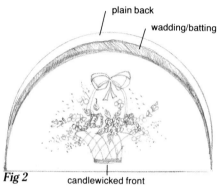

Fig 2

10. Pin, tack and machine stitch around the dome-shaped outline of one half of the tea cosy. Complete the second half in exactly the same way.

11. Gather the lace or broderie anglaise for the frill. Place the frill (with the scalloped edge facing inwards) on the embroidered side of one half of the tea cosy. Pin and tack.

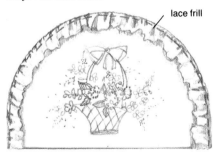

12. Place the second half of the tea cosy on top of the first half, embroidered sides together. Pin the corners together *accurately* and continue to pin towards the dome. Tack, then machine stitch using an overlock stitch or a straight and then a zigzag stitch.

13. Remove tacking threads and trim away any ragged threads. Turn the completed tea cosy right side out.

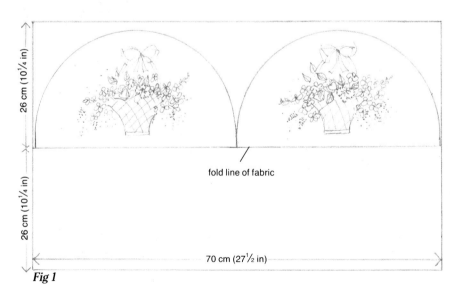

Fig 1

Materials for removable cover

26 cm x 38 cm-wide (10 ¼ in x 15 in-wide) tracing paper

54 cm x 40 cm-wide (21 in x 16 in-wide) fabric for the cover

1.4 m x 3 cm-wide (1 ½ yds x 1 ¼ in-wide) broderie anglaise or lace edging

52 cm x 70 cm-wide (20 ½ in x 27 ½ in-wide) fabric for the lining

52 cm x 35 cm-wide (20 ½ in x 13 ¾ in-wide) medium-weight polyester wadding/batting

1. Fold the tracing paper in half vertically and trace the tea cosy pattern and design on page 76, tracing first one half and then the other to complete the outline and design.

2. Fold the piece of fabric for the cover in half horizontally so that it measures 27 cm x 40 cm (10 ½ in x 16 in) and press. Using the fold as the base line, position the fabric over the tracing and trace the outline and designs onto one half and then onto the other half of the fabric. Do not cut out. (See page 18, fig 3.)

3. Place the fabric in a hoop, positioning the designs in the centre. Stretch the fabric taut and candlewick the designs.

4. When you have completed the candlewicking, remove the fabric from the hoop and refold it. Cut along the outline and fold line. Following the instructions on page 8, wash and iron the candlewicked fabric very well.

5. Make a hem (to the wrong side) along the straight edges of both halves of the tea cosy cover by turning back 5 mm (¼ in) and then another 5 mm (¼ in). Pin, tack and machine stitch.

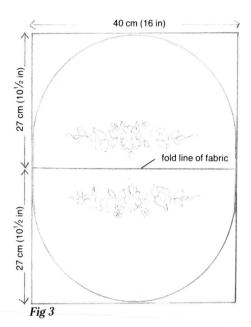

← 40 cm (16 in) →

27 cm (10½ in)

27 cm (10½ in)

fold line of fabric

Fig 3

6. Gather the lace and pin the lace frill (with the scalloped edge facing towards the inside of the tea cosy) to the embroidered side of one half of the tea cosy. Tack the lace into place.

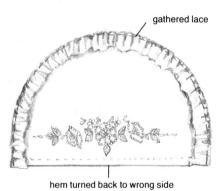

gathered lace

hem turned back to wrong side

7. With right sides together, pin the second half of the tea cosy to the first, beginning at the corners and continuing towards the centre of the dome. Tack, then machine stitch using an overlock stitch or a straight and then a zigzag stitch. Remove the tacking threads and trim away any ragged threads. Turn the tea cosy cover right side out.

8. For the lining, fold the fabric in half horizontally so that it measures 26 cm x 70 cm (10¼ in x 27½ in) and press. This horizontal line becomes the base line of the tea cosy. Open out the fabric and place it on top of the pattern. Matching the base line of the pattern with the fold of the fabric, trace the tea cosy pattern (but not the designs) onto the fabric. Trace a second outline alongside the first as shown in fig 1. Refold the fabric and cut out the two sections of the tea cosy along the outlines, but not along the fold line.

9. Fold the wadding/batting in half horizontally and trace the tea cosy pattern onto it. Cut along both the outline and the fold line.

10. Sandwich a piece of wadding/batting between each of the folded tea cosy shapes. Pin, tack and machine stitch around the dome-shaped outline of each shape.

11. With right sides together, pin the two tea cosy shapes together, beginning at the corners and continuing towards the dome. Tack and machine stitch using an overlock stitch or a straight and then a zigzag stitch. Trim away any ragged threads, remove the tacking and turn the lining right side out. Fit the lining into the embroidered tea cosy cover.

TRAY CLOTH

Materials
46 cm x 35 cm (18 in x 13 ¾ in) fabric
45.5 cm x 35 cm (18 in x 13 ¾ in) polyester wadding/batting (optional)
46 cm x 35 cm (18 in x 13 ¾ in) backing fabric
1.8 m x 3 cm-wide (2 yds x 1 ¼ in-wide) cotton lace

1. Select a suitable design for each end, one of the corners or all four corners and trace it onto one of the pieces of fabric.

2. Place the fabric in the hoop and candlewick the designs. Wash and iron the candlewicked fabric, following the instructions on page 8.

3. If you wish to quilt the design/ designs, tack the wadding/batting to the wrong side of the backing fabric.

4. Turn back (to the wrong side) a 5 mm (¼ in) seam allowance along one short side of both pieces of fabric and press.

5. With right sides together, pin, tack and machine stitch the candlewicked fabric to the backing fabric along the remaining three sides.

6. Clip the corners, remove the tacking threads and turn the tray cloth right side out. Neatly slipstitch the opening closed.

7. If you wish to quilt the tray cloth, follow the instructions for quilting on page 12. Remove the tacking.

8. Machine stitch the lace to the right side of the tray cloth as near to the edge as possible and mitre (page 60) the corners.

APRON

Materials

Tracing paper

48 cm x 47 cm (19 in x 18 ½ in) calico for the apron bib and pocket

1.5 m x 3 cm-wide (1 ¾ yds x 1 ¼ in-wide) lace for bib (optional)

70 cm x 2.5 cm-wide (31 in x 1 in-wide) satin ribbon for the neck string

24 cm x 27 cm (9 ½ in x 10 ½ in) polyester wadding/batting

50 cm x 80 cm (19 ½ in x 31 in) calico for the skirt

2.6 m (2 ⅞ yds) lace for skirt (optional)

Two 60 cm x 5 cm-wide (23 ½ in x 2 in-wide) pieces of calico for the waistband

Two 48 cm x 2.5 cm-wide (19 in x 1 in-wide) satin ribbons for the apron strings

1. Fold a 24 cm x 27 cm-wide (9 ½ in x 10 ½ in) piece of tracing paper in half vertically to measure 24 cm x 13.5 cm (9 ½ in x 5 ⅜ in). Trace the apron bib pattern and design on page 82 onto the tracing paper, completing the pattern and design by tracing first one half and then the other.

2. Trace a 20 cm (8 in) square on tracing paper for the pocket pattern.

3. Fold the fabric for the bib and pocket in half horizontally so that it measures 24 cm x 47 cm (9 ½ in x 18 ½ in) and

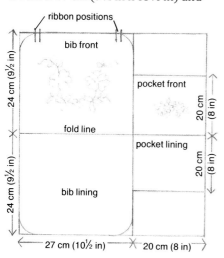

press. Open out the fabric and place it on top of the bib pattern as shown. Matching the bottom line of the pattern with the fold line of the fabric, trace the outline and design onto the fabric. Do not cut out.

4. Trace the pocket pattern onto the same piece of fabric as shown.

5. Place the fabric in the hoop and pull taut. Candlewick the design on the bib. Once the candlewicking is complete, remove the fabric from the hoop and refold. Cut along the outline of the bib and the pocket. Now cut along the fold line of the bib but not the fold line of the pocket. Set the pocket fabric aside.

6. Wash and iron the candlewicked section of the bib, following the instructions on page 8.

7. If you wish to add a lace ruffle to the bib, gather the lace and, with right sides together and matching the raw edge of the bib with the straight edge of the lace, pin the lace into position along three sides as shown below. Tack and machine stitch close to the raw edges.

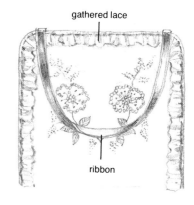

8. Position a loop of 2.5 cm-wide (1 in-wide) ribbon (that goes round the neck) on the bib as shown on page 19 and pin and tack it in place.

9. Tack the wadding/batting to the wrong side of the bib lining. With right sides together, pin the lining and the candlewicked section of the bib together along three sides, leaving the bottom edge open. Tack and machine stitch using an overlock stitch or a straight and then a zigzag stitch. Clip the curves, remove the tacking threads and turn right side out.

10. Prepare the bib for quilting and quilt as described on page 12. Quilt whichever sections of the design you want to accentuate.

11. Tack the open bottom edges together. Remove the tacking done in preparation for quilting.

12. Fold the pocket panel in half and press. This fold line will become the top of the pocket. Turn under (to the wrong side) a 5 mm (¼ in) seam allowance all the way round the other three sides and press.

13. Position the pocket on the right-hand side of the apron skirt fabric and pin, tack and machine stitch it into position.

14. Sew a 1 cm (½ in) hem along both side edges of the skirt fabric and then along the bottom edge.

15. If desired, pin, tack and machine stitch the lace along the sides and bottom of the skirt.

16. Gather the top edge of the skirt until it measures 59 cm (23 ¼ in).

17. With right sides together, pin and tack the raw edge of the bib to the top edge of one of the strips of waistband.

18. Pin and tack the two satin ribbon apron strings in place as shown in the illustration.

19. With right sides together, pin and tack the second strip of waistband to the first strip along the same edge (the bib will be upside down and sandwiched between the two sections of waistband). (See fig 1.)

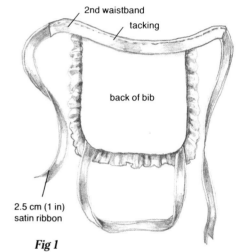

2nd waistband

tacking

back of bib

2.5 cm (1 in) satin ribbon

Fig 1

20. With right sides together, pin the gathered edge of the skirt to the bottom edge of the first waistband, leaving 5 mm (¼ in) as a seam allowance at each end of the waistband. Tack and machine stitch into position.

21. Along the bottom edge of the second strip of waistband turn under (to the wrong side) a 5 mm (¼ in) seam allowance and press.

22. With right sides together, pin the two strips of waistband together along both short sides and tack. Machine stitch along first one short side, then along the tacked long side and finally along the remaining short side. Remove the tacking threads and turn the waistband right side out. (See fig 2.)

23. Pin, tack and slipstitch the opening closed.

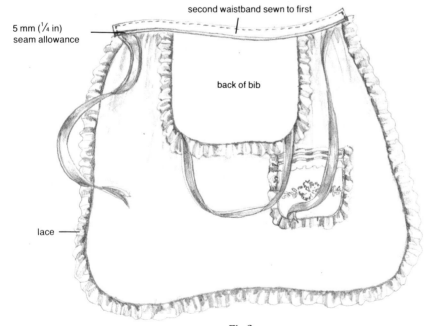

second waistband sewn to first

5 mm (¼ in) seam allowance

back of bib

lace

Fig 2

OVEN GLOVES

Make fully-quilted oven gloves or ones with unquilted pockets and removable pads.

Materials for fully-quilted oven gloves

Tracing paper
18 cm x 88 cm-wide (7 in x 34 ½ in-wide) reversible ready-quilted fabric
50 cm x 40 cm-wide (19 ½ in x 16 in-wide) plain fabric
50 cm x 20 cm-wide (19 ½ in x 8 in-wide) polyester wadding/batting
About 2.2 m (2 ½ yds) bias binding

1. Trace the oven glove pattern on pages 92-93 onto a long piece of tracing paper and cut out the pattern.

2. Fold the quilted fabric in half vertically and pin the long pattern piece to the fabric. Trace the outline onto the fabric.

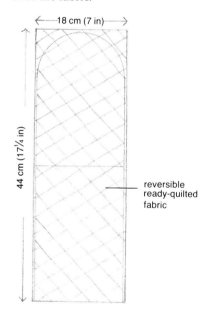

3. Open out the fabric and machine zigzag all the way around the outline. Trim away the excess fabric.

4. Fold the plain fabric in half horizontally so that it measures 25 cm x 40 cm (9 ¾ in x 16 in) and press. Open

out the folded fabric and match the base line of the pocket pattern on page 93 with the fold line of the fabric. Trace the outline and design onto the fabric. Trace another outline and design alongside the first one. Do not cut out.

5. Place the whole piece of fabric in the hoop and pull taut. Candlewick the designs.

6. Refold the fabric and cut along the outlines of the pockets but not along the fold line. Following the instructions on page 8, wash and iron the fabric well.

7. Fold the wadding/batting in half horizontally so that it measures 25 cm x 20 cm (9 ¾ in x 8 in) and pin the pocket pattern to the wadding/batting. Cut along the outline and then along the fold line.

8. Sandwich a piece of wadding/batting between each of the folded sections of candlewicked fabric. Prepare each pocket for quilting and then quilt the designs as described on page 12.

9. Pin, tack and machine stitch the bias binding to the straight edge of each pocket.

10. Match the rounded ends of the long section of the oven gloves with those of the pockets. Pin and tack the pockets into position.

11. Pin, tack and machine stitch the bias binding to the entire outer edge of the oven gloves, making sure that you secure the corners of the pockets properly. Remove the tacking threads.

Materials for oven gloves with removable pads

Tracing paper

18 cm x 88 cm-wide (7 in x 34 ½ in-wide) reversible ready-quilted fabric

50 cm x 40 cm-wide (19 ½ in x 16 in-wide) plain fabric

About 2.2 m (2 ½ yds) bias binding

46 cm x 36 cm-wide (18 in x 14 in-wide) calico for the pads

46 cm x 18 cm-wide (18 in x 7 in-wide) polyester wadding/batting

1. Trace the pattern on pages 92-93 onto a long piece of paper and cut out the pattern. Fold the quilted fabric in half vertically so that it measures 18 cm x 44 cm (7 in x 17 ½ in). Pin the pattern piece to the fabric. Trace the outline.

2. Open out the fabric, machine zigzag all round the marked outline, then trim away the excess fabric.

3. Fold the plain fabric in half horizontally so that it measures 25 cm x 40 cm (9 ¾ in x 16 in) and press. Open out the fabric and position the straight edge of the pocket pattern on the fold line of the fabric. Trace the outline and design onto the fabric. Trace another outline and design alongside the first. Do not cut out.

4. Place the fabric in a hoop and pull taut. Now candlewick the designs.

5. Refold the fabric and cut along the outlines of the pocket, but not along the fold. Wash and iron the candlewicked fabric well, following the instructions on page 8.

6. Refold the pockets and pin the bias binding to the straight edge of each pocket. Tack and machine stitch.

7. Match the rounded ends of the long section of the oven gloves with those of the pockets and pin and tack the pockets into position.

8. Pin, tack and machine stitch the bias binding to the entire outer edge of the oven gloves, making sure that the corners of the pockets are secure.

9. To make the separate pads, fold the calico in half horizontally so that it measures 23 cm x 36 cm (9 in x 14 in) and press.

10. Pin the pocket pattern to the fabric, matching the straight edge of the pattern with the fold line of the fabric. Trace the outline, then trace a second outline alongside the first.

11. Cut along the outline, then along the fold of each pocket.

12. Turn back (to the wrong side) and press a 1 cm (½ in) seam allowance along all four straight bottom edges.

13. With right sides together, pin and tack two pieces of fabric together. Machine stitch around the raw edges, leaving the straight bottom edge open. Sew the other two pieces together in the same way. Clip the curves, remove the tacking and turn the fabric right side out.

14. Fold the wadding/batting in half horizontally and pin the pocket pattern to the folded wadding/batting. Cut along the outline and then along the fold of the wadding/batting.

15. Slip one piece of wadding/batting into each pad and slipstitch the opening closed.

16. Slip the pads into the pockets of the oven gloves.

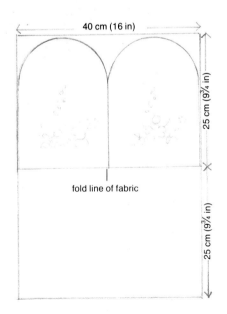

40 cm (16 in)

25 cm (9¾ in)

fold line of fabric

25 cm (9¾ in)

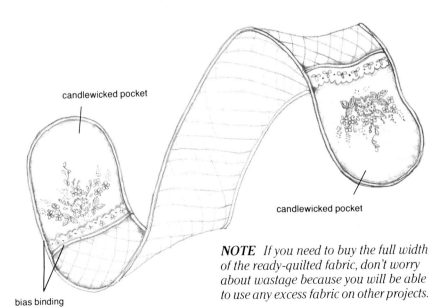

candlewicked pocket

candlewicked pocket

bias binding

NOTE *If you need to buy the full width of the ready-quilted fabric, don't worry about wastage because you will be able to use any excess fabric on other projects.*

RUFFLED COTTAGE CURTAINS

As windows come in many shapes and sizes, it is impossible to include a list of requirements, but remember that cottage curtains need to be gathered very full and to hang just below sill length to look their best.

TO CALCULATE THE WIDTH AND THE LENGTH OF THE CURTAINS

To calculate the length, measure from the curtain rail (rod) or track to the windowsill and add on 15 cm (6 in) [which will include a 3 cm (1¼ in) turnback at the top of the curtain and a 2 cm (⅞ in) bottom seam allowance]. A 9 cm (3½ in) or 10 cm (4 in) fabric or lace ruffle will be added to this measurement and the curtains will hang approximately 20 cm (8 in) below the windowsill when finished. If the window is positioned just above the kitchen sink, adjust the length accordingly so that the curtain and ruffle do not hang near the taps.

To calculate the width, measure the length of the rail (rod) and at the very least double the measurement. When using preshrunk calico as curtain fabric (unlined), it is preferable to triple the measurement. Divide the double (or triple) measurement in half to give the width measurement for each of the two curtains.

OTHER MATERIALS NEEDED

HEADING (RUFFLETTE) TAPE If you use standard heading (rufflette) tape you will need the same width as the curtains plus about 2 cm (⅞ in) extra *per* curtain for the turnbacks.

LACE OR FABRIC RUFFLE To calculate how much lace or fabric ruffle you will need *per curtain,* measure the length plus the width of the curtain and double

the measurement. (Refer to the Box on page 62 for hints on how to make ruffles.)

TIE-BACKS Loop the tape measure around the curtain as if it were a tie-back. The measurement of the loop is the length of the finished tie-back. Add a 2 cm (⅞ in) seam allowance and cut a piece of fabric the required length by 48 cm (19 in) wide. You will also need two pieces of iron-on vilene interfacing

measuring the finished length of each panel with a width of 11 cm (4¼ in).

VALANCE You will need triple the measurement of the rail (rod) by 42 cm (16½ in) for the valance. Cut as many widths as required, each with a depth of 42 cm (16½ in) and join the widths using French seams (see steps 11-13).

1. *To make the curtains,* begin by pulling a thread across the width of the material to act as a guide when cutting the edge of the curtains straight. This is very important, otherwise the curtains will not hang correctly.

2. Cut the number of drops (widths) that you need and cut off the selvedges to prevent puckering.

3. If you need to join widths, do so as neatly as possible because with the light shining through the curtains from behind, untidy seams will be very noticeable. (I always use French seams - see steps 11-13 below.)

4. Choose a design to candlewick in one corner of each curtain or perhaps as a border and trace the design onto the fabric.

5. Place the fabric into a hoop and stretch taut. Candlewick the designs, then wash and iron the fabric well as directed on page 8.

6. Trim away ragged threads, as once again, any untidiness will show up with the light shining through the curtains from behind.

7. Once the candlewicking is complete, make the curtains. Make a hem on one side edge only (the side furthest away from the candlewicking) of the curtain by turning under first 1 cm (½ in) and then 2 cm (⅞ in). Pin, tack and machine stitch using a straight stitch.

8. Turn back 3 cm (1¼ in), to the wrong side, along the top edge of the curtain, then press and tack.

9. Gather the preboiled and ironed lace (see preparation of cotton lace, page 8) or fabric ruffle (page 62) and pull up the gathers until it measures the same as the combined length and width measurement of one curtain.

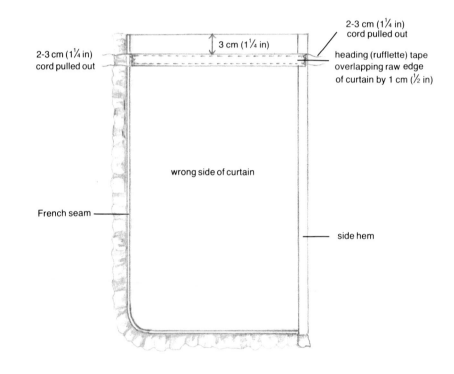

2-3 cm (1¼ in) cord pulled out

3 cm (1¼ in)

2-3 cm (1¼ in) cord pulled out

heading (rufflette) tape overlapping raw edge of curtain by 1 cm (½ in)

wrong side of curtain

French seam

side hem

10. Make a hem (to the wrong side) along both short ends of the lace or ruffle and machine stitch.

11. With *wrong sides* together, pin together the straight edge of the gathered lace and the raw edge of curtain, starting at the top of the curtain.

12. Tack and machine stitch using an overlock stitch or a straight and then a zigzag stitch.

13. Now with right sides together, and adjusting the gathers so that they lie straight, pin and tack a slightly wider seam than before (French seam). Machine stitch using a straight stitch. Press the seam back towards the curtain.

14. Pull out 2-3 cm (⅞-1¼ in) of cord from both ends of the heading (rufflette) tape and knot the cord ends together at one end.

15. Turn under 1 cm (½ in) to the wrong side at each end of the heading (rufflette) tape. Pin the tape to the curtain, overlapping the raw edge of the curtain by 1 cm (½ in). Tack and machine stitch close to the edges of the tape, using a straight stitch. Remember to sew along the short ends of the tape as well.

16. Pull up the cord until the curtain fits the window, then roll up the long end of the cord so that it looks tidy. Do not cut this long length of cord.

17. Complete the other curtain in exactly the same way.

18. *To make a valance* (which may also be candlewicked if you wish), turn back 5 mm (¼ in) and then 1 cm (½ in) along the bottom edge of the valance to make a hem. Make a hem exactly the same way along both side edges of the fabric. Pin, tack and machine stitch using a straight stitch.

19. If desired, first stitch lace (having first made a small hem on both short ends of the lace) along the bottom edge of the valance, then stitch ribbon just above the inside edge of the lace.

20. Turn back 1 cm (½ in) and then 9 cm (3½ in) to the wrong side along the top of the valance. Press. Pin, tack and machine stitch close to the edge of the seam allowance.

21. Push the wooden rod through the casing you made at the top of the valance and hang the rod on the wooden brackets.

22. *For the tie-backs,* draw four panels, each 12 cm (4¾ in) wide, on the fabric. Two of the panels are to be candle-wicked and two are for the lining.

23. Trace the candlewick designs on page 67 onto two of the panels in the positions indicated in the illustration.

24. Place the fabric in the hoop and pull taut. Candlewick the designs.

25. Cut out the four panels and wash and iron the two candlewicked panels very well, following the directions on page 8.

26. Cut two pieces of iron-on vilene interfacing equal to the finished length of each panel with the width measuring 11 cm (4¼ in). Centre the vilene interfacing on each piece of lining and pin it in place, leaving a 5 mm (¼ in) seam allowance all round the edges. Iron the vilene onto each panel so that the vilene becomes bonded to the fabric.

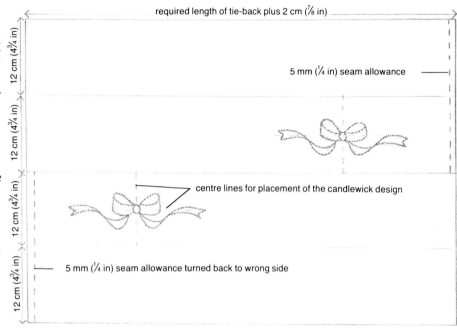

required length of tie-back plus 2 cm (⅞ in)

12 cm (4¾ in)

12 cm (4¾ in)

12 cm (4¾ in)

12 cm (4¾ in)

5 mm (¼ in) seam allowance

centre lines for placement of the candlewick design

5 mm (¼ in) seam allowance turned back to wrong side

27. Turn back, to the wrong side, a 5 mm (¼ in) seam allowance along one short side of each of the four panels and press.

28. With right sides together (the embroidery to the inside) pin a candlewicked panel to one piece of lining. Tack and machine stitch along the remaining short side and two long sides, clip the corners, then turn the fabric right side out. Slipstitch the opening closed and press.

29. Repeat with remaining candlewicked panel and lining.

30. Sew a small brass ring to the centre of both ends of each strip so that the tie-backs can be hooked onto small hooks screwed into the wall at the side of the curtains.

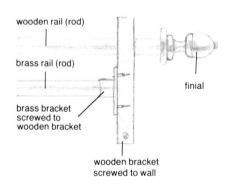

wooden rail (rod)

brass rail (rod)

finial

brass bracket screwed to wooden bracket

wooden bracket screwed to wall

NOTE *You can purchase brass or chrome-plated rods and brackets (from which you will hang the curtains), which should be screwed to the inside edge of the wooden brackets, leaving sufficient space to allow the curtains to be drawn freely.*

THE NURSERY

As a child, I grew up on a smallholding surrounded by open fields and tree-clad mountains. We had a lovely stream running through the bottom of our garden and it was there that I spent many happy hours in a make-believe world. Woodland animals, rocking horses and hearts are but a few of the magical memories of my childhood that I have incorporated into the designs used in this fantasy nursery.

CAROUSEL MOBILE

Materials

Six 40 cm x 40 cm (16 in x 16 in) pieces plain or different coloured felt

Three 40 cm x 1 cm-wide (16 in x ½ in-wide) satin ribbons, each a different colour

Three 45 cm x 1 cm-wide (18 in x ½ in-wide) satin ribbons, each a different colour

Polyester stuffing or potpourri

Wooden or brass curtain ring

Inside hoop of a 30 cm (12 in) embroidery hoop

Glue

2 m (2 ⅛ yds) scalloped cotton lace or broderie anglaise

Seven satin bows

Two small bells

1. Trace the designs on pages 74, 75 and 81 onto the felt, following the directions for tracing a design on page 9. Draw the outline of each design *twice*, remembering that each animal must face to the left and to the right. *Do not cut out.*

2. Place each piece of felt in the hoop and pull taut. Candlewick around the inside outline and any other features, for example faces, manes and tails.

3. Once all the candlewicking is complete, cut out all the animals and hearts along their cutting lines. With *wrong* sides together, pin both sections of each animal and heart together.

4. Insert one end of a length of satin ribbon into each animal and heart and secure. Using the foot of your sewing machine as a guide, stitch around the outline of each shape, leaving a 3 cm (1¼ in) opening along one side.

5. Stuff each shape with polyester stuffing or potpourri. Neatly stitch the opening closed.

6. Tie the other end of each ribbon to the wooden or brass curtain ring.

7. Mark each ribbon 30 cm (12 in) from the curtain ring. Mark the outside of the hoop at 16 cm (6½ in) intervals and apply glue to the wooden hoop at these points. Apply glue to the dull side of each ribbon at the 30 cm (12 in) mark. Allow the glue on both surfaces to become tacky and then press each ribbon very firmly against the outside of the hoop at the points where you applied the glue.

8. Gather the lace or broderie anglaise and sew the two ends together. Pull up the gathers to fit around the outside of the hoop and glue the lace to the hoop.

9. Glue a bow to the hoop between each ribbon. Tie a bow and two bells to the base of the wooden or brass ring.

NURSERY TIDY

Materials

Two 61 cm x 76 cm (24 in x 30 in) pieces calico or other background fabric
Four 20 cm x 2.5 cm-wide (8 in x 1 in-wide) ribbons for hanging the tidy
120 cm x 6 cm-wide (1⅜ yds x 2½ in-wide) contrasting fabric for elastic casing
62 cm x 2 cm-wide (24½ in x ⅞ in-wide) elastic
120 cm x 40 cm (1⅜ yds x 16 in) contrasting fabric for pockets
62 cm (24 ½ in) narrow elastic
61 cm x 76 cm (24 in x 30 in) polyester wadding/batting
About 2.2 m (2½ yds) bias binding
Satin bow
Curtain rod or dowel

1. Round off the two bottom corners of the two pieces of calico or other plain-coloured fabric.

2. Trace the designs on pages 94-95 to fit the top 27 cm (10½ in) of one piece of calico as shown in the illustration.

3. Candlewick the designs and when complete, wash and iron the fabric well, following the instructions on page 8.

4. Fold the four ribbons in half (wrong sides together) and match their raw edges with that of the fabric. Pin and tack them in position as shown.

5. To make the elastic casing, fold the piece of contrasting fabric in half lengthways. With right sides together, stitch a 5 mm (¼ in) seam along the long raw edge. Turn the fabric right side out.

6. Draw a line across the width of the candlewicked fabric, 27 cm (10½ in) from the top raw edge. Mark the line at 10 cm (4 in) intervals. Mark the elastic casing at 20 cm (8 in) intervals.

7. Thread the wider elastic through the casing and pin both ends to the sides of the tidy at the 27 cm (10½ in) line. Match the marks on the casing with those on

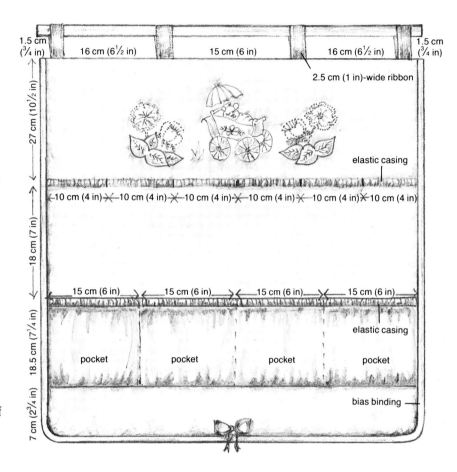

the line and machine stitch securely. Sew the loose ends of the elastic and casing to the side edges of the candlewicked fabric.

8. Draw a horizontal line right across the width of the tidy 18 cm (7 in) below the casing. Draw another line 18.5 cm (7¼ in) below that line. Mark both lines vertically at 15 cm (6 in) intervals.

9. Fold the fabric for the pockets in half lengthways so that it measures 120 cm x 20 cm (1⅜ yds x 8 in) and press. Make marks 2.5 cm (1 in) long and 30 cm (12 in) apart along both long edges of the folded pocket fabric.

10. Open out the fabric and gather along the fold line. Pull up the gathers so that the fabric measures 60 cm (24 in) across.

11. Matching the marks on the fold line of the pocket fabric with those on the bottom line on the tidy, pin the gathered fabric to the background fabric. Machine stitch into place.

12. Bring the two raw edges together again and tack. Fold under 5 mm (¼ in) and then 1.5 cm (¾ in) to the wrong side to make a casing for the narrow elastic. Pin, tack and machine stitch. Thread the narrow elastic through the casing.

13. Match the marks along the casing with those on the second line on the background fabric and pin into place.

14. Stitch vertical lines between the marks on the second and third lines.

15. Tack the raw side edges of the pockets to the background fabric. You will now have four separate pockets.

16. Place the backing (lining) fabric and then the wadding/batting on top of the candlewicked side of the tidy. [The four ribbon loops will now be sandwiched between the candlewicked fabric and the backing (lining) fabric.] Matching the raw edges, pin, tack and machine stitch along the top edge, then turn the backing fabric and wadding/batting towards the back. The ribbon loops will now be the right way up.

17. Pin all three layers together around the other three sides and tack. Turn back 5 mm (¼ in) on both ends of the bias binding and pin the binding to the front of the tidy around these three sides. Tack and machine stitch, making sure that you catch the ends of the elastic, casing and pockets. Fold the bias binding (over the raw edge) towards the back of the tidy and pin. Tack and then slipstitch the bias binding in place.

18. If you wish to quilt the candlewick design, prepare to quilt and quilt as described on page 12. Remove tacking stitches.

19. Sew a pretty satin ribbon bow to the bottom of the tidy. Hang the loops of satin ribbon on the curtain rod or dowel.

20. If desired, make four extra felt animals (see Mobile page 28) and hang two from satin loops, on either side of the dowel or rod.

THE COT QUILT

As cot quilts require frequent washing, choose a fabric that launders well. Should you wish to use a pure cotton, wash it well first to prevent shrinkage. A cot quilt candlewicked in colour looks very pretty but you can use a plain, coloured fabric and candlewick the designs using cream or coloured thread.

Materials for a cot quilt with a finished size of 75 cm x 110 cm (29 ¾ in x 43 ½ in)
Two 76 cm x 111 cm (30 in x 43 ¾ in) pieces calico or other fabric
About 3 m (3 ¼ yds) preboiled cotton lace (see page 8)
Two 90 cm (35 in) satin ribbons
Two 126 cm (49 ½ in) satin ribbons
75 cm x 110 cm (29 ¾ in x 43½ in) thin polyester wadding/batting

1. Trace the designs on pages 94-95 and place them together to form the complete design. Use sticky tape at the back of the designs to hold them together.

2. Fold one piece of calico in half vertically and then in half horizontally. Press. Open out the fabric and match the centre lines of the fabric with those of the design. Trace the design onto the fabric.

3. Place the fabric in the hoop and pull taut. As it is rather a large design begin candlewicking in the centre of the design and work your way towards the outside.

4. Once you have finished the candlewicking, wash and iron the fabric very well, following the instructions on page 8. This will be the last time you iron the fabric.

5. Mark off 13 cm (5 ¼ in) from the outside edges all the way round the quilt. Pin the straight edge of the preboiled insertion lace (see page 8 for preparation of lace) along this line all

the way round the quilt, mitring the corners (page 60).

6. Tack and machine stitch the lace in place.

7. Pin, tack and machine stitch all the way round the outer edge of the lace.

8. Leaving a 20 cm (8 in) loose length at either end of each of the four satin ribbons, pin the ribbons along the inside edges of the lace as shown in the illustration overleaf. Make sure that the

edge of the ribbon slightly overlaps the edge of the lace.

9. Tack and machine stitch along both edges of each of the lengths of ribbon, stopping about 1 cm (½ in) away from each of the corners.

10. Tie bows at each corner of the design.

11. Turn back a 5 mm (¼ in) seam allowance along one short side of both pieces of fabric. Finger-press.

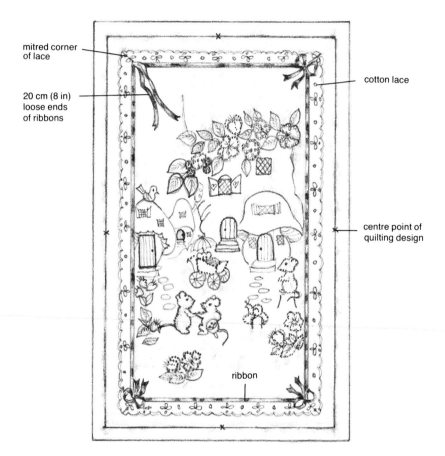

mitred corner
of lace

20 cm (8 in)
loose ends
of ribbons

cotton lace

centre point of
quilting design

ribbon

WALL-HANGING

A colourful, pretty wall-hanging will
brighten up any room and is
particularly lovely in a child's room.
There are several ways of completing a
wall-hanging - the simplest being to use
an embroidery hoop as a frame.

Materials
40 cm x 40 cm (16 in x 16 in) calico or
other plain fabric for background
30 cm (12 in) embroidery hoop for the
frame
40 cm x 40 cm (16 in x 16 in) thin
polyester wadding/batting
40 cm x 40 cm (16 in x 16 in) muslin
2.5 m (2 ¾ yds) preboiled lace of
desired width (page 8)

1. Fold the calico in half vertically and
then in half horizontally. Finger-press.
Open out the fabric and match the
centre lines of the fabric with those of
the design on page 81. Trace the design
onto the fabric.

2. Place the fabric in the embroidery
hoop and pull taut. Candlewick the
design.

3. Wash and iron the completed design
very well, following the instructions on
page 8.

12. Trace the quilting design onto the
border of the quilt, beginning the design
at the points marked x and working
towards the corners.

13. With right sides together and raw
edges matching, pin and tack the
candlewicked front to the lining along
three sides of the quilt. Machine stitch
with an overlock stitch or a straight
stitch and then zigzag stitch, leaving an
opening along the side where you
turned back the seam allowance.

14. Clip the corners and turn the quilt
right side out.

15. Slip the wadding/batting inside,
working the corners of the wadding/
batting into the corners of the quilt.
Slipstitch the opening closed.

16. Prepare the quilt for quilting by
following the instructions on page 12.
Quilt all those parts of the design that
you wish to accentuate. Quilt the
border, as well as along the inside edge
of the ribbon and the outside edge of
the lace. This will give the border a
more quilted effect.

17. Remove the tacking threads.

4. Sandwich the wadding/batting
between the candlewicked square and
the muslin. Prepare for quilting and
quilt as described on page 12.

5. Gather the lace (see page 8 for
preparation of cotton lace) until it
measures 103 cm (1 ⅛ yds). Place the
candlewicked and quilted fabric in the
hoop and pull fairly taut.

6. Draw a line with a water-erasable pen
close to and around the bottom edge of
the hoop. Remove the fabric from the
hoop and add on an extra 6 mm (¼ in)
all round the circumference. Trim away
the excess fabric.

7. With right sides together (and the scalloped edge of the lace lying towards the centre of the circle) pin the straight edge of the gathered lace to the raw edge of the circle. Tack, then machine stitch the lace into place using an overlock stitch.

8. Join the two short ends of the lace together by sewing a French seam (page 24, steps 11-13). Trim away any ragged threads and remove the tacking.

9. Centre the candlewicked circle over the inner wooden hoop. Replace the outer wooden hoop and tighten the screw securely. Pull the fabric fairly taut and adjust the lace ruffles so that they will lie flat when the wall-hanging is hung against the wall.

10. Sew a loop of ribbon to the back of the ruffle so that the wall-hanging can hang from a hook or nail.

11. If desired, the back of the wall-hanging can be neatened. Cut a circle of fabric or felt the same size as the inner hoop and zigzag around the outer edge. Glue the fabric to the back of the inner hoop.

THE BATHROOM

Delicate candlewick embroidery enhances guest towels, a toilet seat cover, toilet roll holder and tissue box holder. A cream on cream candlewicked bath mat provides a contrast to the more colourful items. Whether you prefer the neutral look of cream embroidery on calico or the brighter hues of pinks and greens, candlewicked bathroom accessories will harmonize with both contemporary and old-fashioned bathrooms. This often neglected area of your home can be made to look attractive and comfortable with the addition of these eye-catching articles.

TOILET SEAT COVER

Materials

41 cm x 41 cm (16½ in x 16½ in) calico
41 cm x 41 cm (16½ in x 16½ in) calico for lining
41 cm x 41 cm (16½ in x 16½ in) polyester wadding/batting
2-3 m (2¼-3¼ yds) preboiled cotton lace or broderie anglaise
98 cm x 10 cm-wide (1⅛ yds x 4 in-wide) calico for casing
About 30 cm (12 in) bias binding
Narrow elastic
Two 20 cm (8 in) satin ribbons

1. Take a piece of newspaper and place it between the toilet seat and lid. Trace the outline of the lid. Add 1.5 cm (¾ in) all the way round the circumference.

2. Now measure the pattern for the toilet seat lid horizontally and vertically. This will determine how much fabric you will need. For a standard toilet seat lid, the measurements given above under **Materials** should be sufficient.

3. Pin the pattern of the toilet seat lid to the fabric and trace the outline. Do likewise with the lining. Do not cut out as it will not fit into the hoop properly.

4. Find the centre lines of the toilet seat cover by folding the outline in half vertically and then horizontally. Press.

5. Match the centre lines of the fabric with those of the design and trace the design onto one piece of fabric. Place in the hoop and pull taut. Candlewick the design.

6. Once the candlewicking is complete, cut along the outlines on both pieces of fabric and wash and iron the candlewicked fabric.

7. Cut a piece of wadding/batting exactly the same size and sandwich it between the candlewicked fabric and the lining. Prepare for quilting and quilt the design as described on page 12.

8. Measure the circumference of the pattern of the toilet seat lid and double the measurement, adding on a 3 cm (1¼ in) seam allowance. This will determine the length of lace required.

9. Gather the lace to fit around the circumference of the cover. With right sides together, position the lace on the toilet seat cover with the scalloped edge facing towards the centre. Leaving a 3 cm (1¼ in) loose end, pin, tack and machine stitch the lace in place. When you reach the place where you began, make a French seam on the lace as follows: With *wrong* sides of the lace together, pin and machine stitch a 5 mm (¼ in) seam. Turn the lace so that *right* sides are together and stitch a slightly wider seam than before. Stitch the lace to the cover.

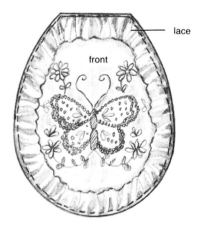

lace

front

10. Make a seam at either end of the long piece of calico. For the casing for the elastic, turn back 5 mm (¼ in) and then 1.5 cm (¾ in) to the wrong side along one long side. Pin, tack and machine stitch.

11. With right sides together, pin this long strip to the candlewicked side of the toilet seat cover. (The lace or broderie anglaise will be sandwiched between the candlewicked side and the long strip of calico.) Machine stitch in place. Remove tacking threads.

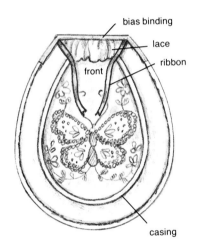

12. Place the bias binding as indicated in the illustration and sew it into position.

13. Turn the seat cover right side out and thread the elastic through the casing, pulling the elastic up until the cover fits the toilet seat lid securely. Secure the ends of the elastic to the casing with several rows of stitching.

14. Stitch the satin ribbon to either end of the casing as shown.

TOILET ROLL HOLDER

For this project, cut a piece of fabric wide enough to be placed in an embroidery or quilting hoop. Once the candlewick embroidery is completed, the excess fabric will be cut away and can be used for another project.

Materials
106 cm x 40 cm-wide (42 in x 16 in-wide) calico
26 cm x 2.5 cm-wide (10¼ in x 1 in-wide) satin ribbon
Brass ring

1. On the left-hand side of the calico, mark off a panel 106 cm x 24 cm (42 in x 9½ in) wide. Ignore the extra fabric on the right-hand side as you will cut it off after you have candlewicked the design.

2. Fold the 24 cm x 106 cm (9½ in x 42 in) panel in half vertically and press along this line.

3. Place the top right-hand section of the panel (G) on top of the design on page 75 and trace the design.

4. Place the fabric in a hoop and pull taut. Candlewick the design, then cut off the 106 cm x 24 cm (42 in x 9½ in) panel. Wash and iron the whole panel

but particularly concentrate on the candlewicked portion (see page 8).

5. Thread the ribbon through a brass ring, bring the ends together and secure.

6. Place the folded satin ribbon in position as shown (AA-BB) and tack in place.

7. Turn back, to the wrong side, a 1 cm (½ in) seam allowance along the bottom edge of the panel.

8. With right sides together, (the candlewicking will be to the inside) refold the panel vertically and pin the raw edges together along the top and side edges. Machine stitch along the top and side seams and clip the corners. Turn the panel right side out and neatly slipstitch the bottom edge closed. Press.

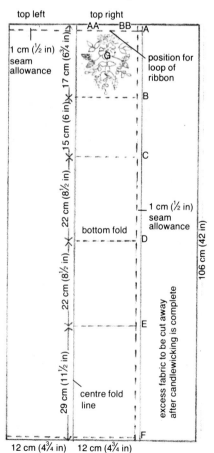

top left   top right

1 cm (½ in) seam allowance

position for loop of ribbon

17 cm (6¾ in)

15 cm (6 in)

22 cm (8½ in)

1 cm (½ in) seam allowance

22 cm (8½ in)

bottom fold

29 cm (11½ in)

centre fold line

excess fabric to be cut away after candlewicking is complete

106 cm (42 in)

12 cm (4¾ in)   12 cm (4¾ in)

9. From the top edge (A) measure and mark off 17 cm (6¾ in) (B). From (B) measure and mark off 15 cm (6 in) (C). From (C) measure and mark off 22 cm (8½ in) (D) which becomes the bottom fold line. From (D) measure and mark off 22 cm (8½ in) (E). From (E) measure and mark off 29 cm (11½ in) (F).

10. Pin (E) to (C) and (F) to (B) on the front of the toilet roll holder. Tack and sew right across the width of the fabric. You will now have a holder with two loops in which to insert two toilet rolls.

11. If desired, hang two candlewicked hearts stuffed with potpourri from the brass ring and tie a pretty bow to the base of the brass ring.

BATH MAT

Materials
82 cm x 56 cm (32 in x 22 in) fabric
82 cm x 56 cm (32 in x 22 in) fabric for lining
82 cm x 56 cm (32 in x 22 in) polyester wadding/batting
Ribbon and lace

1. Fold one piece of fabric in half horizontally and then vertically to determine the centre point. Match the centre point of the fabric with those of the design and trace the design onto the fabric.

NOTE It is important to use a central design as the quilting will anchor the three layers (candlewicked top, wadding/batting and lining) and prevent the bath mat bunching in the middle.

2. Place the fabric in a hoop and pull taut. Candlewick the design and then wash and iron the fabric very well, following the directions on page 8.

3. If you wish to decorate the bath mat with lace and ribbon, do so at this stage. There are many ways in which you can decorate the bath mat but if you wish to make the one featured here, first pin, tack and sew on all the lace as shown in the illustration.

4. Position each length of ribbon so that one edge overlaps the edge of the lace slightly and hides the machine stitching on the lace. Pin, tack and machine stitch the lengths of ribbon in place.

5. Turn back, to the wrong side, a 5 mm (¼ in) seam allowance along one short side of both the front and back sections of the bath mat. Press.

6. Tack the wadding/batting to the wrong side of the lining. With right sides together, pin, tack and machine stitch the candlewicked front of the bath mat to the lining along the other short side and both long sides, using an overlock stitch or a straight and then a zigzag stitch.

7. Clip the corners, remove tacking threads and turn the bath mat right side out. Neatly slipstitch the opening closed.

8. Prepare the mat for quilting and quilt as described on page 12. You may also wish to quilt along the edge of the ribbon (closest to the candlewicking design) and along the edge of the lace. Remove the tacking stitches.

TISSUE BOX HOLDER

Materials
Tracing paper
42 cm x 52 cm-wide (16½ in x 20½ in-wide) calico
42 cm x 26 cm-wide (16½ in x 10¼ in-wide) thin polyester wadding/batting
20 cm x 26 cm-wide (8 in x 10¼ in-wide) calico for the inset
20 cm x 13 cm-wide (8 in x 5¼ in-wide) thin polyester wadding/batting
Four 20 cm (8 in) satin ribbons
1.6 m (1¾ yds) bias binding

1. Fold the tracing paper in half vertically. Align the fold line with the centre fold line of the pattern on page 80. Trace all the details including the design onto the tracing paper. Do the same for the inset (page 81).

2. Cut along the traced outlines, turn the folded pattern pieces over and complete the other half of the design and details. Open out the tracing paper.

3. Fold the 42 cm x 52 cm-wide (16¼ x 20½ in) fabric in half horizontally to measure 21 cm x 52 cm (8¼ in x 20½ in) and finger-press. Place the bottom fold line of the tissue box holder pattern on the fold of the fabric, pin the pattern to the fabric and trace around the outline.

4. Turn the fabric over and hold it up to a windowpane. Trace the outline of the pattern on the back to correspond with the outline on the front.

5. For the lining, trace a second outline on the front of the fabric alongside the first but do not turn the fabric over as you did in Step 4.

6. Open out the fabric and place it on top of the pattern, matching the outline on the fabric with that of the pattern. Trace the design. Turn the fabric around and trace the design onto the other half of the outline. *Do not cut out.*

7. Place the fabric in a hoop and stretch taut. Candlewick the design on the front half, remove the fabric from the hoop and place the second design to be candlewicked in the hoop and pull taut. Candlewick the second design.

8. Refold the fabric and cut along the outlines of both the candlewicked fabric and the lining. Wash and iron the candlewicked section carefully.

9. Fold the 42 cm x 26 cm-wide (16½ in x 10¼ in-wide) wadding/batting in half horizontally to measure 21 cm x 26 cm (8¼ in x 10¼ in). Place the bottom fold line of the pattern on the fold of the wadding/batting. Pin and cut out.

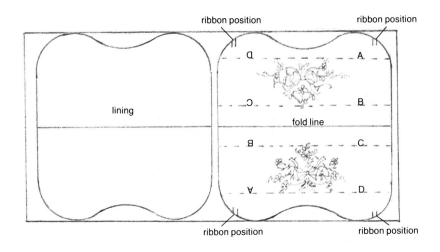

10. Place this wadding/batting between the candlewicked fabric and the lining. Prepare the fabric for quilting and quilt as described on page 12.

11. Fold the second piece of fabric in half horizontally so that it measures 10 cm x 26 cm (4 in x 10¼ in). Pin the inset pattern piece with the curved bottom fold line on the fold of the fabric. Trace around the outline. Trace another outline alongside the first. Cut along first one outline and then the other.

12. Fold the 20 cm x 13 cm-wide (8 in x 5¼ in-wide) wadding/batting in half horizontally to measure 10 cm x 13 cm (4 in x 5¼ in). Place the inset pattern piece on the wadding/batting, pin and then cut out. Cut along the fold line. [You will now have two pieces of wadding/batting 10 cm x 13 cm (4 in x 5¼ in).]

13. Sandwich a piece of wadding/batting between each folded inset piece. Pin, tack and machine stitch close to the raw edges of first one inset and then the other.

14. Pin the bias binding to the long straight edge of each inset. Tack and machine stitch using a straight stitch.

15. *To assemble the tissue box holder:* with wrong sides together pin the left top corner of the inset to the main section of the tissue box holder at (A). Pin the left bottom curved corner to (B), the right curved corner to (C) and the top right corner to (D).

16. Tack from (A) to (D) and machine stitch in place, easing the straight edge of the main section of the holder round the curved corners of the inset.

17. Pin, tack and machine stitch the second inset to the main section of the tissue box holder in the same way.

18. Tack the ribbons in the positions indicated on the illustration.

19. Turn back 5 mm (¼ in) to the wrong side along the short end of the bias binding and finger-press. Beginning in an inconspicuous place, pin the bias binding all around the outer edge of the tissue box holder. When you return to where you began, overlap the turned back beginning of the bias binding by 1 cm (½ in). Machine stitch the bias binding in position.

20. Fold the bias binding over the raw edges and tack in position. Hand sew the binding in position, using a blind hem stitch. Remove tacking.

21. Place the box of tissues in the completed tissue holder and tie the satin ribbons either end into bows.

GUEST TOWELS

Hand-embroidered guest towels are lovely to look at and a pleasure to use in one's own home. They also make wonderful gifts. Should you wish to make a really special gift, use huckaback, Irish or Belgian linen, as these are the traditional fabrics used for fine guest towels. You may, of course, use terry towelling or a purchased guest towel for a less expensive version. Whichever fabric you use, ensure that it is both easily washable and absorbent.

Materials for one guest towel
40 cm x 40 cm (16 in x 16 in) fabric for the candlewicked panel
33 cm x 8 cm (13 in x 3¼ in) very thin polyester wadding/batting (optional)
53 cm x 33 cm (21 in x 13 in) linen, huckaback or towelling
Two 33 cm x 8 mm-wide (13 in x ⅜ in-wide) satin ribbons
33 cm (13 in) cotton lace or broderie anglaise

1. *If you are making your own guest towel,* draw a rectangle 33 cm x 8 cm (13 in x 3¼ in) wide onto the fabric for the candlewicked panel.

2. Find the centre lines of the panel by folding the rectangle in half vertically and then horizontally. Press the folds.

3. Open out the fabric and match these lines with the centre lines of the design on page 91. Trace the design onto the panel.

4. Do not cut out the panel as it will then be too small to fit in the hoop. Place the fabric in a hoop and pull taut. Now candlewick the design.

5. Stitch around the outside edges of the panel using a zigzag stitch and cut it out. Wash and iron the panel carefully, following the instructions on page 8.

6. If you wish to quilt the panel, cut a piece of the thinnest wadding/batting available the same size as the panel.

7. With a water-erasable pen, draw a line 8 cm (3¼ in) from the bottom raw edge of the towel and position the bottom edge of the wadding/batting and the candlewicked panel on this line. Pin both layers to the towel.

8. Tack and machine stitch close to the raw edges of the panel.

9. Prepare the panel for quilting and quilt as described on page 12.

10. Zigzag the short ends of the panel to the towel as close to the raw edges as possible.

11. Pin a strip of satin ribbon to the edge of each long side of the panel, so that the ribbon overlaps the panel and hides the machine stitching.

12. Tack and machine stitch the ribbon into place.

13. Make a hem along both the long sides of the towel by turning under 5 mm (¼ in) and then 1 cm (½ in) to the wrong side. Pin, tack and machine stitch using a straight stitch.

14. Make a hem in the same way along the top and bottom edges of the towel.

15. Machine stitch cotton lace or broderie anglaise to the bottom hem of the towel.

16. Remove the tacking threads.

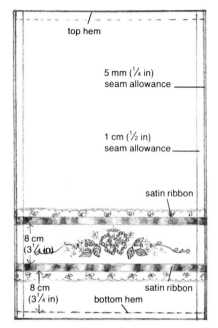

top hem

5 mm ($\frac{1}{4}$ in)
seam allowance

1 cm ($\frac{1}{2}$ in)
seam allowance

satin ribbon

8 cm
(3$\frac{1}{4}$ in)

8 cm
(3$\frac{1}{4}$ in)   satin ribbon

bottom hem

1. *If you are using a purchased guest towel,* measure the width of the towel and draw a rectangle 8 cm (3$\frac{1}{4}$ in) wide x the width of the towel onto the fabric for the candlewicked panel. Add an extra 2 cm ($\frac{7}{8}$ in) to the length of the panel to allow for the seam allowance.

2. Find the centre lines of the panel by folding the rectangle in half vertically and then horizontally. Press the folds.

3. Open out the fabric and match these lines with the centre lines of the design on page 91. Trace the design onto the panel.

4. Do not cut out the panel as it will then be too small to fit in the hoop. Place the fabric in a hoop and pull taut. Candlewick the design.

5. Stitch around the outside edges of the panel using a zigzag stitch and cut it out. Wash and iron the panel carefully, following the instructions on page 8.

6. Turn back to the wrong side a 1 cm ($\frac{1}{2}$ in) seam allowance on both short sides of the panel. Press.

7. If you wish to quilt the panel, cut a piece of the thinnest wadding/batting available the same size as the panel.

8. With a water-erasable pen, draw a line 6 cm (2$\frac{1}{2}$ in) from the bottom hem of the towel and position the bottom edge of the wadding/batting and the candlewicked panel on this line. Pin both layers to the towel.

9. Tack and machine stitch along the two long edges close to the raw edges of the panel.

10. Tack, then slipstitch the side edges.

11. Prepare the panel for quilting and quilt as described on page 12.

12. Turn under 1 cm ($\frac{1}{2}$ in) at both ends of each satin ribbon.

13. Pin a length of ribbon to the edge of each long side of the panel, so that the ribbon overlaps the panel and hides the machine stitching.

14. Tack and machine stitch the ribbon into place. Slipstitch the short ends in place.

15. Stitch cotton lace or broderie anglaise to the bottom hem of the towel. Remember to make a narrow hem on both short ends of the lace.

16. Remove the tacking threads.

THE BEDROOM

With their neutral tones and simple designs, candlewicked handicrafts blend well with almost any style of décor, but it is in romantic, soft-furnished interiors that they really come into their own. This cottagey bedroom has a delightfully old-fashioned mood that evokes strong feelings of nostalgia. The pale cream colour scheme is offset by the warm tones of wood and thatch, while a juxtaposition of different fabrics – cotton, calico, ribbon, lace and linen – introduces interesting textural contrasts. Precious heirloom quilts, cushions and bed linen, enhanced by decorative candlewick embroidery, add to the tranquil country setting.

QUILTS

Before beginning work on your quilt, read very carefully through the general instructions and the two methods of assembling a quilt. This is essential, as it will help you to determine what size squares are to be cut out.

TRADITIONAL METHOD Should you wish to make a traditional quilt, where each square is framed by lace and the quilt has both horizontal and vertical sashing, the squares will be smaller.

EASIER METHOD However, should you prefer a simpler way of completing the quilt, you can sew all the squares together without any sashing in between. The squares, therefore, must be proportionately larger to make up for the lack of sashing. The lace is then sewn on top of the seams.

To determine the overall dimensions of the quilt
Before you can work out the number and size of the squares, you will need to work out the exact dimensions of the quilt for your particular bed. In order to do this you must first measure the mattress:

1. Measure the *width* of the mattress and add on twice the depth. Add on an extra 30 cm (12 in) to allow for an overhang of 15 cm (6 in) either side of the mattress.

2. Measure the *length* of the mattress and add on twice the depth. Add an extra 15 cm (6 in) to allow for an overhang at the foot of the bed. As one normally uses a valance (nightfrill) on the base of the bed, the quilt needs to hang 15 cm (6 in) longer than the mattress only on three sides of the bed (not at the top end).

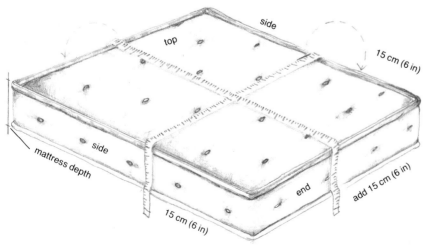

Easy method   top border

side border

side border

bottom border   squares sewn together without sashing

NOTE If your bed has both a footboard and a headboard, it would not be necessary to add an extra 15 cm (6 in) to the length measurement.

CONVENTIONAL BED SIZES

To determine the number and size of the squares for your quilt, consult the tables (pages 56-57) for quilts with sashing (the vertical and horizontal strips between the squares) and for those without. The calculations are based on the measurements of a modern innerspring mattress with a depth of about 18 cm (7 in) and cover many of the popular sizes of mattresses available.

Cutting out squares, borders and sashing
Before cutting out the squares, add on an extra *2 cm (⅞ in)* per square. For example, if the measurement of the square given in the table above is 45 cm (17 ½ in), add on an extra 2 cm (⅞ in). The size of the square you will cut out will be 47 cm x 47 cm (18 ½ in x 18 ½ in). This extra 2 cm (⅞ in) includes a 6 mm (¼ in) seam allowance and allows for shrinking and puckering of the fabric.

At a later stage, once you have completed the candlewicking, the squares will be washed and then blocked (cut exactly square).

Add on an extra *2 cm (⅞ in)* to the width of each piece of sashing and an extra *2 cm (⅞ in)* to the width of each border.

UNCONVENTIONAL BED SIZES

You may find that the measurements of your mattress and, therefore, the size of your quilt, do not conform with those given in the tables on pages 56-57.

If this is the case, refer to the tables and select the quilt size closest to the one you require. It is preferable to choose a quilt that is too large rather than too small for your bed.

However, you may wish to try to calculate the size of the squares yourself, as detailed below.

To calculate the size of the squares for a quilt with sashing
Once you have measured the mattress and determined the overall size of the quilt required for your particular bed, do the following calculation:

From the full width measurement, subtract twice the width of the border [e.g. 2 x 30 cm (2 x 12 in)] plus twice the width of the sashing [e.g. 2 x 10 cm (2 x 4 in)]. (You will see in the illustration on page 44 that there are only two lots of sashing in the width of a quilt made up of twelve squares.) Now divide by three (there are three squares in the width).

Subtract twice the width of the border [e.g. 2 x 30 cm (2 x 12 in)] plus three times the width of the sashing [e.g. 3 x 10 cm (3 x 4 in)] from the full length measurement. (The illustration on page 44 shows three lots of sashing in the length.) Now divide this total by four (there are four squares in the length).

For example, if you have calculated that you require a 200 cm x 250 cm (80 in x 100 in) quilt for your double bed, subtract as follows:

Width measurement   200 cm/80 in
subtract sashing
 (e.g. 2 x 10 cm/4 in)   20 cm/ 8 in
                       =   180 cm/72 in

subtract borders
 (e.g. 2 x 30 cm/12 in)   60 cm/24 in
                     =   120 cm/48 in
divide by three   =   40 cm/16 in

Length measurement = 250 cm/100 in
subtract sashing
 (e.g. 3 x 10 cm/4 in)   30 cm/12 in
                     =   220 cm/88 in

subtract borders
 (e.g. 2 x 30 cm/12 in)   60 cm/24 in
                     =   160 cm/64 in
divide by four   =   40 cm/16 in

You require twelve 40 cm x 40 cm (16 in x 16 in) fabric squares to make this quilt.

These particular measurements happened to work out exactly but very often they do not. Remember that the width of the sashing and borders is fairly flexible and can either be reduced or enlarged or the sashing can be left out altogether.

NOTE The width measurement of the horizontal sashing must equal that of the vertical sashing. The width of the borders, too, must be uniform throughout.

To calculate the size of the squares for a quilt without sashing
In order to get the above calculations to work, you will only need to subtract twice the width of the borders from the width measurement and twice the width of the borders from the length measurement.

For example, if the double bed quilt you want to make measures 200 cm x 250 cm (80 in x 100 in), work out the size of the squares as follows:

Width measurement   =   200 cm/80 in
subtract borders
 (e.g. 2 x 25 cm/10 in)   50 cm/20 in
                     =   150 cm/60 in
divide by 3   =   50 cm/20 in

Length measurement = 250 cm/100 in
subtract borders
 (e.g. 2 x 25 cm/10 in)   50 cm/ 20 in
                     =   200 cm/80 in
divide by 4   =   50 cm/ 20 in

This quilt will consist of twelve 50 cm x 50 cm (20 in x 20 in) squares with borders 25 cm (10 in) wide.

NOTE If your calculations to determine the size of the squares (whether for a quilt with sashing or for one without sashing) do not work out, try dividing the length measurement by five instead of four. If this works out, you will then need to make a quilt with fifteen rather than twelve squares.

Remember to add on the extra 2 cm (⅞ in) to the measurement of each square and an extra 2 cm (⅞ in) to the width measurement of each border before cutting them out.

QUILT WITH SASHING

Materials for 200 cm x 250 cm (80 in x 100 in) double-bed quilt with sashing
10 m x 150 cm-wide (11 yds x 60 in-wide) or 12 m x 120 cm-wide (13 yds x 48 in-wide) calico for the squares, sashing, borders and backing
20-22 m x 7 cm-wide (21½-24 m x 2¾ in-wide) lace
214 cm x 264 cm (84½ in x 104 in) thin polyester wadding/batting
Crochet cotton or embroidery thread

1. Prepare the fabric for the quilt as described on page 8.

2. Follow the instructions on page 44 for measuring the mattress. Refer to the tables of quilt measurements on pages 56-57 and select the size quilt that will fit your particular bed. Remember to add on an extra 2 cm (⅞ in) to all the measurements given to allow for shrinkage and puckering. A 6 mm (¼ in) seam allowance is included.

3. Cut out the number of squares, plus enough fabric for the sashing and borders required for your quilt. Cut the vertical sashing and all the borders a little longer than the finished length and width of the quilt. Cut the horizontal sashing the full width of the fabric but do not cut it into short lengths yet. Always pull a thread, do not tear the material, as this will stretch the edges and make the assembling of the quilt more difficult.

4. Prepare the cotton lace as described on page 8.

5. Trace the designs onto the calico squares, centring them accurately as described on page 9. Any inaccuracy will be apparent once the quilt is complete.

NOTE Accuracy is most important at all stages of making a quilt, as it will save you a great deal of time when you assemble your quilt.

6. Place each calico square in turn in the hoop and stretch the fabric taut.

7. Select the threads you enjoyed using on your sampler and candlewick the designs.

    HINT The marks made by the water-erasable pen can be removed at this stage by dipping the squares in plain, lukewarm water and hanging them up to dry.

8. When you have candlewicked *all* the squares, wash them all plus the fabric for the sashing and the borders, in the same soapy water. Wash each square very carefully, making quite sure that you have removed the ring marks that the hoop might have made, as well as any other dirty marks.

NOTE *It is very important that all dirty marks are removed during this wash. If any of the squares need to be washed a second time, they will become a shade lighter than the rest of the squares. This will spoil the overall look of your quilt.*

9. Rinse all the fabric in plain water and then use a fabric softener.

10. Wrap each square individually in a towel and squeeze dry. Do the same for the fabric required for the sashing and borders. Do not hang out to dry.

11. Place a thick towel, (not an embossed one) folded double, on the ironing board. Put each square, candlewicked side down, on the towel and iron it carefully. Do not use too hot an iron as it might scorch the fabric.

12. Always iron the sashing and borders lengthways to ensure an even width throughout.

To block the squares
13. The tension of your work and the ironing will have altered the original size of the squares and it is important that they are all the same size. Measure each square horizontally and vertically to determine which is the smallest. Use graph paper (this is the only reliable way of making a template) to make an accurate template of the measurement of the smallest square. Paste this template onto fairly stiff cardboard or an x-ray plate and cut it out carefully.

14. Find and mark with a water-erasable pen the centre point of the sides of the template and of each fabric square.

15. Place the fabric square on a smooth table surface. *Do not stretch* the edges of the fabric square, even if the thread has shrunk and pulled the square out of alignment. *Smooth* the edges and stick the fabric square to the table with tape. Line up the centre points of the template with those of the square, draw round the edge of the template and cut

out. Your fabric square should now be a perfect square.

To assemble the quilt
16. Lay the horizontal sashing on the table and, using the same template as before, mark and cut the sashing to the correct size. These will become the short pieces of sashing to be sewn between the squares. The edges of your sashing and the fabric squares will be exactly the same length.

17. If you wish to frame each square with lace, cut the lace exactly the same width or length as the square (you can use the same template as you used to block the squares and short sashing). Make sure that the pattern of the lace is balanced at both ends (that is, that it doesn't stop halfway through a pattern on one side and not on the other). Cut four pieces of lace for each square.

18. Pin, tack and sew the lace to the top and bottom of each square and then to the sides, stitching about 2-3 mm (⅛ in) from the raw edge of the square and 2-3 mm (⅛ in) from the inner edge of each strip of lace. Tack the raw ends of the lace to the edges of the fabric. Complete all 12 squares in exactly the same way.

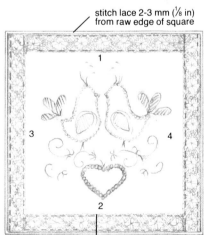

stitch lace 2-3 mm (⅛ in) from raw edge of square

stitch inside edge of lace to squares

19. Lay out the completed squares in the desired positions.

20. Trace the quilting designs onto all the short pieces of horizontal sashing (see page 48, step 28) before you assemble the quilt. Matching the bottom corners of a square with the top corners of a piece of sashing, pin from the centre to the corners. Ease, tack and sew, using the foot of your machine as a guide (in this way, the row of stitching on the lace will not be visible as it will be sewn to the inside of the seam).

21. Sew the top of the next square to the bottom edge of the sashing. Continue in this manner until you have sewn the first panel of four squares. Now assemble the second panel of four squares and then the third. You will now have three panels of four squares.

1st square

1st sashing

2nd square

2nd sashing

3rd square

3rd sashing

4th square

22. To strengthen the seams, overlock them all or use a straight stitch and then a zigzag stitch. Press all the seams towards the squares.

23. Trace the quilting designs onto both pieces of vertical sashing (see step 28).

NOTE *Following the next few instructions carefully will make all the difference as to whether all the corners line up accurately or not.*

24. To assemble, first measure the distance between where the sewing machine needle enters the fabric when using a straight stitch and the raw edge of the square. This measurement will be about 6 mm (¼ in), depending on the make of your machine, and will be the seam allowance for all your seams.

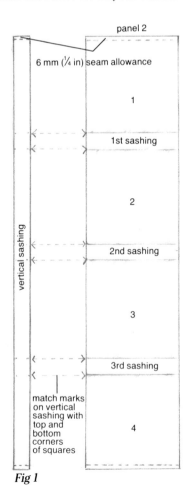

Fig 1

25. Draw this 6 mm (¼ in) seam allowance right across the top end of both pieces of vertical sashing and the first square of each of the three panels. Take the measurement from the 6 mm (¼ in) mark at the top left-hand corner of the first square to the bottom left-hand corner of this same square. Take another measurement from the bottom left-hand corner of the first square to the bottom left-hand corner of the first strip of horizontal sashing. Mark these measurements on a long strip of paper. Now, starting from the 6 mm (¼ in) mark at the top end of the vertical sashing, mark off these two measurements all the way down both sides of both pieces of vertical sashing. (See fig 1)

26. Matching these marks with the corners of the squares, pin the three panels to the two pieces of vertical sashing. Tack and machine stitch using an overlock stitch or a straight and then a zigzag stitch.

27. Measure the front of the quilt across the width and cut out the top and bottom borders slightly longer than this measurement. Measure the length of the quilt and add on the width of the top and bottom borders [that is an extra 60 cm (24 in)]. Cut out the side borders slightly longer than this measurement.

28. Trace the quilting design onto the four border pieces, beginning at the centre point of each border and working out towards the corners. This will prevent having an incomplete design at one end and a complete design at the other end of the border. (See fig 2)

29. Pin, tack and sew the borders to the squares, beginning with the top and bottom borders and then the sides. Overlock these seams and give the completed front of the quilt a final pressing. Do not press the borders with a steam-iron if you have used a water-erasable pen to trace the quilting design as any steam or water will erase it.

To attach the wadding/batting and backing fabric
30. Measure the completed quilt front and cut the wadding/batting and backing fabric approximately 5-7 cm (2-2¾ in) wider on all four sides than the quilt top. [In other words you will add 10-14 cm (4-5½ in) to the length and 10-14 cm (4-5½ in) to the width.]

31. Place the backing fabric on the floor, centre the wadding/batting over it and smooth it out. Now lay the quilt front (candlewicked side uppermost) on top of the wadding/batting. Make quite sure that you straighten out any creases in the backing and wadding/batting before you start to pin (you may need the help of a friend).

32. Pin all three layers together, beginning in the centre and working your way out towards the centre of the outside edges. Then pin from the centre to each corner.

33. Using a strong thread, tack along these pinned lines and between each of these lines. Continue to tack until you have done *at least* 32 rows of tacking. It really is worth the effort. The more you tack, the easier it is to quilt because the wadding/batting does not shift as much (see page 12).

34. Quilt the 12 candlewicked squares, starting from the centre of the quilt and working your way towards the outside edges and corners. (See page 12 on quilting.) Smooth any excess fullness toward the edges as you work.

35. Quilt the horizontal and vertical sashing and finally, the borders.

NOTE *When quilting the sashings and the borders, always start at the centre point of each piece and work towards the corners/edges.*

36. Once you have completed the quilting of the borders, trim the excess wadding/batting and backing so that it is the same width all the way around the

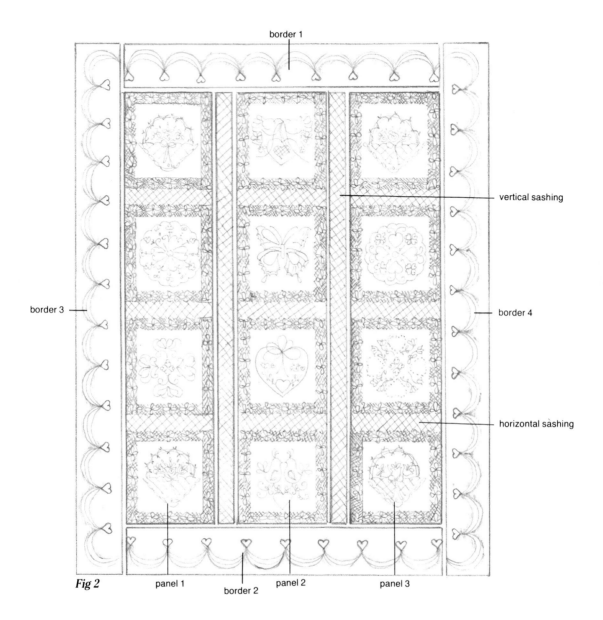

border 1

vertical sashing

border 3

border 4

horizontal sashing

Fig 2 panel 1 panel 2 panel 3

border 2

quilt. Turn the raw edges of the backing approximately 2 cm (⁷⁄₈ in) to the wrong side (towards the wadding/batting) and press.

37. Now fold the backing fabric over the quilt front to create a self-binding. Begin with the top and bottom edges first and then the side edges. Pin, tack and slipstitch into place. To make sure that the wadding/batting is held firmly in place, quilt close to the hem that has just been made. Remove all the tacking threads.

QUILT WITHOUT SASHING

This method is much quicker and easier than the first method and is by far the more suitable for a beginner. Whether you use the first or second method, you are sure to be delighted with the finished quilt. As mentioned before, it will be necessary to make the squares proportionately larger to make up for the lack of sashing.

Materials for 204 cm x 252 cm (80 in x 100 in) double-bed quilt without sashing
10 m x 150 cm-wide (11 yds x 60 cm-wide) or 12 m x 120 cm-wide (13 yds x 48 in-wide) calico for squares, borders and backing
About 16 m x 5-9 cm-wide (18 yds x 2-3½ in-wide) lace
266 cm x 218 cm (104 in x 86 in) polyester wadding/batting

1. Prepare the fabric for the quilt as described on page 8.

2. Follow the instructions on page 44 for measuring the mattress. Refer to the tables of quilt measurements on pages 56-57 and select the size quilt that will fit your particular bed. Add on an extra 2 cm (⅞ in) to all the measurements given to allow for shrinkage and puckering. A 6 mm (¼ in) seam allowance is included.

3. Cut out the number of squares required for your quilt. Cut the borders a little longer than the finished width and length of the quilt [that is 204 cm (80 in) and 252 cm (100 in)]. Always pull a thread, do not tear the material as this will stretch the edges, making it more difficult to assemble the quilt.

4. Prepare the cotton lace as described on page 8.

5. Trace the designs onto the squares, centring them accurately as described on page 9 as any inaccuracy will be apparent once the quilt is complete.

6. Place each calico square in turn in the hoop and stretch the fabric taut.

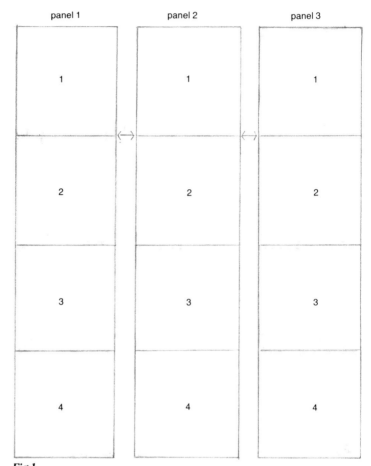

Fig 1

7. Select the threads you enjoyed using on your sampler and candlewick the designs.

HINT The marks made by the water-erasable pen can be removed at this stage by dipping the squares in *plain* lukewarm water and hanging them up to dry.

8. When you have candlewicked all the squares, wash them all plus the fabric for the borders and backing, in the same soapy water. Wash each square very carefully, making quite sure that you have removed the ringmarks that the hoop might have made, as well as any other dirty marks.

9. Rinse all the fabric in plain water and then use a fabric softener.

10. Wrap each square individually in a towel and squeeze dry. Do the same for the fabric required for the borders. Do not hang out to dry.

11. Place a thick towel, (not an embossed one) folded double, on the ironing board. Put each square, candlewicked side down, on the towel and iron it carefully. Do not use too hot an iron as it might scorch the fabric.

12. Iron the borders lengthways to ensure an even width throughout.

To block the squares
13. The tension of your work and the ironing will have altered the original size of your squares and it is important that they are all cut the same size. Measure each square horizontally and

vertically to determine which is the smallest. Use graph paper to make an accurate template of the measurement of the smallest square. Paste this template onto fairly stiff cardboard or an x-ray plate and cut it out carefully.

14. Find and mark with a water-erasable pen the centre point of the sides of the template and of each fabric square.

15. Place the fabric square on a smooth table surface. *Do not stretch* the edges of the fabric, even if the thread has shrunk and pulled the square out of alignment. *Smooth* the edges and stick the fabric square to the table with sticky tape. Line up the centre points of the template with those of the square, draw around the edge of the template and cut out.

The embroidered fabric should now be a perfect square.

To assemble the quilt
16. Lay out the squares in the desired positions. Now sew the squares together in three panels of four squares as shown in the illustration. Overlock all the seams and press them so that they all lie in the same direction.

17. Placing two panels right sides together, match the corners, pin, tack and sew. Sew panel 1 to panel 2 and panel 2 to panel 3. Overlock the seams and press. (See fig 1.)

18. Measure the front of the quilt across the width and cut out the top and bottom borders slightly longer than this measurement. Measure the length of the quilt and then add on the width of the top and bottom borders [that is an extra 60 cm (24 in)]. Cut out the side borders slightly longer than this measurement.

19. Cut three lengths of lace a little longer than the width of the quilt (before the borders are sewn on), making sure that the pattern is balanced at both ends of the lace. Match the centre lines of the lace with the three horizontal seam lines and pin the lace to the fabric. Tack and sew into place.

20. Cut two lengths of lace a little longer than the length of the quilt (before the borders are sewn on), again making sure that the pattern is balanced at both ends of the lace. Match the centre lines of the lace with the two vertical seam lines and pin the lace to the fabric as shown opposite. Tack and sew the lace into place.

21. Tack the raw ends of the lace to the edges of the fabric.

22. Sew on the top and bottom borders of the quilt and then the two side borders. Press.

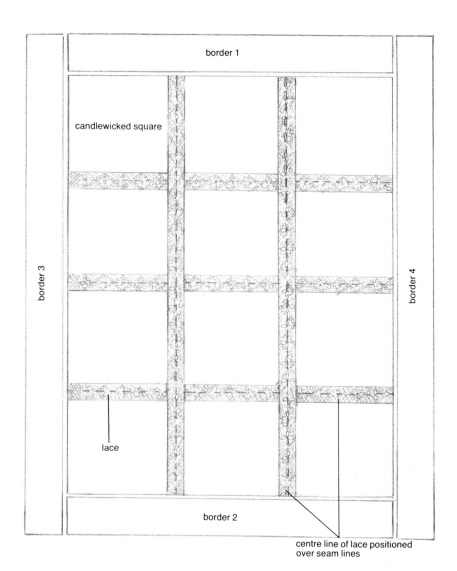

border 1

candlewicked square

border 3

border 4

lace

border 2

centre line of lace positioned over seam lines

23. Pin on the lace that frames the entire central section of the quilt in the position shown in the illustration. Mitre the corners, tack and sew into place.

24. Trace the quilting designs onto the four borders, beginning in the centre of each and working towards the corners.

To attach the wadding/batting and backing fabric
25. Measure the completed quilt front and cut the wadding/batting and backing fabric approximately 5-7 cm (2-2¾ in) wider on all four sides than the quilt top. [In other words you will add 10-14 cm (4-5½ in) to the length and 10-14 cm (4-5½ in) to the width.]

26. Place the backing fabric on the floor, centre the wadding/batting over it and smooth it out. Now lay the quilt front (candlewicked side uppermost) on top of the wadding/batting. Make quite sure that you straighten out any creases in the backing and wadding/batting before you start to pin (you may need the help of a friend).

27. Pin all three layers together, beginning in the centre and working your way out towards the centre of the outside edges. Pin from the centre to each corner.

28. Using a strong thread, tack along these pinned lines and between each of these lines. Continue to tack until you have done at least 32 rows of tacking. The more you tack, the easier it is to quilt because the wadding/batting does not shift as much (see page 12).

29. Quilt the 12 candlewicked squares, starting from the centre of the quilt and working your way towards the outside edges and corners. (See page 12 on quilting.) Smooth any excess fullness toward the edges as you work.

30. Quilt the borders, beginning the quilting at the centre point of each border and working towards the corners. Once you have completed the quilting of the borders, trim the excess wadding/batting and backing so

that it is the same width all the way round the quilt.

31. Turn the raw edges of the backing 2 cm (⅞ in) to the wrong side and press. Now fold the backing fabric over the quilt front to create a self-binding. Begin with the top and bottom edges first and then the side edges. Pin, tack and slipstitch into place. To ensure that the wadding/batting is held firmly in place, quilt close to the hem that has been made. Remove tacking threads.

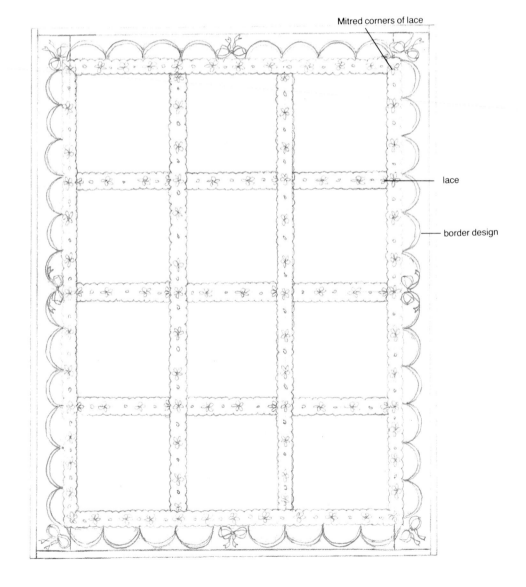

Mitred corners of lace

lace

border design

BED LINEN

Making your own candlewicked sheets and pillowcases is a very easy project to begin with, as you can make your own by buying sheeting from a fabric shop. Alternatively, you can buy ready-made sheets and pillowcases that only need to be candlewicked.

SHEETS AND PILLOWCASES

Materials for a sheet
Ready-made sheet or sheeting (see Box on page 55)
Scalloped cotton edging lace or broderie anglaise
Satin ribbon

1. In order to position the candlewick design on page 69 accurately, [or any other design measuring approximately 5 cm (2 in) in depth], it is necessary to find the centre lines of the sheeting. On the right side of the fabric, measure

13 cm (5 in) from the top raw edge and draw a line parallel to the raw edge. Fold the sheet in half lengthways to find the vertical centre line. Finger-press about 20 cm (8 in) along this vertical fold line, starting at the raw edge.

2. Match the centre lines of the design with the centre lines of the sheeting and trace the design onto the right side of the fabric.

3. Stretch the sheeting in an embroidery hoop and candlewick the design.

4. Make a hem along the raw edge by turning under 1 cm (½ in) and press. Now turn under a further 8 cm (3¼ in) to the wrong side. Pin, tack and machine stitch. This wide hem will enclose the wrong side of the candlewicking so that the sheet looks neat.

5. Stitch the edging lace or broderie anglaise to the right side of the edge of the hem to make the sheet look pretty and feminine.

6. To determine the length of each satin ribbon, measure the width of the sheet and add on 2 cm (⅞ in). Stitch the

ribbons in position as shown in the photograph.

7. Make the bottom hem by turning under 1 cm (½ in) and then 2 cm (¾ in) to the wrong side. Pin, tack and machine stitch.

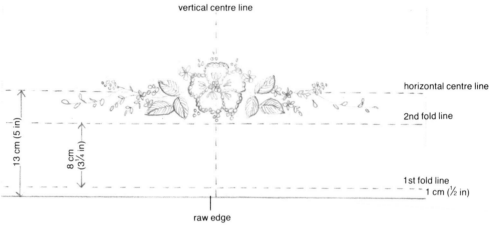

vertical centre line

horizontal centre line

2nd fold line

13 cm (5 in)

8 cm (3¼ in)

1st fold line
1 cm (½ in)

raw edge

PILLOWCASES

Materials for two pillowcases with lace ruffles
1 m x 200 cm-wide (1⅛ yds x 78 in-wide) sheeting
About 10 m x 9 cm-wide (10¾ yds x 3½ in-wide) cotton lace or broderie anglaise

1. Cut the sheeting into four 50 cm x 72 cm (19½ in x 28 in) pieces for the pillowcases and two 50 cm x 22.5 cm (19½ in x 8¾ in) pieces for the flaps. (See fig 1 opposite.)

2. Trace the designs on page 75 and 77 onto tracing paper. This will make inverting the designs much easier.

3. Match the outside edges of the pattern with those of the fabric and trace the design onto as many of the corners as you wish to candlewick.

4. Place the fabric in the hoop and candlewick the designs. Once you have completed the candlewicking, wash and iron the fabric very well, following the instructions on page 8.

5. Prepare the lace as described on page 8. Cut the lace into two equal lengths and gather by hand or machine. Most machine-made lace has one slightly thicker thread fairly close to the straight edge. Find this thread, pull it gently to gather the lace easily. If you prefer to gather the lace by machine, set the machine on the longest stitch, loosen the top tension slightly and work two rows of stitching fairly close to the straight edge of the lace. Pull both threads carefully at the same time and gather to the required length. Reset your machine to the normal stitch length.

6. Pin the gathered lace, right sides and raw edges together, to the front of the pillowcase. Leaving about 3 cm (1¼ in) of loose gathered lace at each end, machine stitch the lace in place. When you are 2-3 cm (⅞-1¼ in) from the first corner, leave the needle in the fabric, lift the presser foot and push as much of the gathered lace as you can under it. Release the presser foot and stitch until you get to about 6 mm (¼ in) from the corner. Again leave the needle in the fabric and lift the presser foot. Turn the

fabric and push as much gathered lace as possible under the foot. Release the presser foot and continue machine stitching. Repeat this process at each corner.

7. When you reach the point where you started, release the presser foot and cut the thread. With *wrong* sides of the lace together, pin and machine stitch a 5 mm (¼ in) seam. Now turn the lace so that *right* sides are together and stitch a slightly wider seam than before. This is called a French seam and is a neat way of finishing off any visible seams. Machine stitch the ruffle to the fabric.

8. Turn under 5 mm (¼ in) and then 1 cm (½ in) along one long side of one of the flaps. Pin, tack and machine stitch.

9. With right sides together, pin and tack the other long side of the flap to one of the short sides of the candlewicked front.

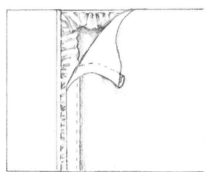

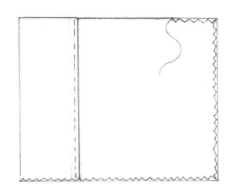

10. Open out the flap so that it lies away from the candlewicked front. Turn under 5 mm (¼ in) and then 1 cm (½ in) along one short side of the fabric for the

back of the pillowcase. Pin, tack and machine stitch.

11. With right sides together, pin and tack the other three sides of the back to the front (the lace will be sandwiched between the two layers).

12. Return the flap, and pin and tack in place.

13. Machine stitch around all four sides through all thicknesses using a straight and then a zigzag or an overlock stitch.

14. Remove tacking threads and turn the pillowcase right side out.

15. Repeat steps 6-14 for the second pillowcase.

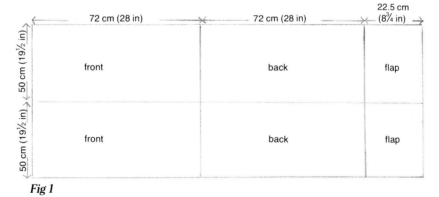

Fig 1

To calculate the amount of fabric needed to make a sheet.
Measure the width of the mattress and add on twice the depth. Add on about 40 cm (16 in) to allow one to tuck in the sheet. Use sheeting that has a width closest to this measurement to avoid having to sew hems on these two sides.
    Measure the length and add on twice the depth. Remember to add on the 40 cm (16 in) tuck-in allowance.

To calculate the fabric required for a pillowcase.
Measure the width and length of the pillow and add on a 1 cm (½ in) seam allowance all round. Cut two pieces of fabric this size. Cut another piece of fabric the same width measurement x 20 cm (8 in).
    If you are making a plain pillowcase without a ruffle, cut the fabric all in one piece from very wide sheeting.

To calculate the fabric required for the ruffle.
Measure the circumference of the pillow and double the measurement. Add on 1.5 cm (¾ in) for seam allowances. The width of the ruffle is flexible but remember to add 2.5 cm (1 in) to the width measurement for the hem (of a fabric ruffle) and seam allowances.

QUILTS WITH SASHING

SINGLE-BED QUILT (12 Squares)

QUILT SIZE*	No. of squares	×	Size of squares	+	No. of sashings	×	Width of sashings	+	No. of borders	×	Width of borders
Width 181 cm (71 in)	3	×	37 cm (14½ in)	+	2	×	10 cm (4 in)	+	2	×	25 cm (9¾ in)
Length 228 cm (89½ in)	4	×	37 cm (14½ in)	+	3	×	10 cm (4 in)	+	2	×	25 cm (9¾ in)
Width 190 cm (75½ in)	3	×	40 cm (16 in)	+	2	×	10 cm (4 in)	+	2	×	25 cm (9¾ in)
Length 240 cm (95½ in)	4	×	40 cm (16 in)	+	3	×	10 cm (4 in)	+	2	×	25 cm (9¾ in)

SINGLE-BED QUILT (15 Squares)

QUILT SIZE*	No. of squares	×	Size of squares	+	No. of sashings	×	Width of sashings	+	No. of borders	×	Width of borders
Width 160 cm (63½ in)	3	×	30 cm (12 in)	+	2	×	10 cm (4 in)	+	2	×	25 cm (9¾ in)
Length 240 cm (95½ in)	5	×	30 cm (12 in)	+	4	×	10 cm (4 in)	+	2	×	25 cm (9¾ in)
Width 165 cm (65¼ in)	3	×	35 cm (13¾ in)	+	2	×	10 cm (4 in)	+	2	×	20 cm (8 in)
Length 255 cm (100¾ in)	5	×	35 cm (13¾ in)	+	4	×	10 cm (4 in)	+	2	×	20 cm (8 in)

DOUBLE-BED QUILT (12 Squares)

QUILT SIZE*	No. of squares	×	Size of squares	+	No. of sashings	×	Width of sashings	+	No. of borders	×	Width of borders
Width 195 cm (76½ in)	3	×	45 cm (17½ in)	+	2	×	10 cm (4 in)	+	2	×	20 cm (8 in)
Length 250 cm (98 in)	4	×	45 cm (17½ in)	+	3	×	10 cm (4 in)	+	2	×	20 cm (8 in)
Width 200 cm (80 in)	3	×	40 cm (16 in)	+	2	×	10 cm (4 in)	+	2	×	30 cm (12 in)
Length 250 cm (100 in)	4	×	40 cm (16 in)	+	3	×	10 cm (4 in)	+	2	×	30 cm (12 in)

QUEEN-SIZE BED QUILT (16 Squares)

QUILT SIZE*	No. of squares	×	Size of squares	+	No. of sashings	×	Width of sashings	+	No. of borders	×	Width of borders
Width 250 cm (98 in)	4	×	45 cm (17½ in)	+	3	×	10 cm (4 in)	+	2	×	20 cm (8 in)
Length 250 cm (98 in)	4	×	45 cm (17½ in)	+	3	×	10 cm (4 in)	+	2	×	20 cm (8 in)
Width 250 cm (100 in)	4	×	40 cm (16 in)	+	3	×	10 cm (4 in)	+	2	×	30 cm (12 in)
Length 250 cm (100 in)	4	×	40 cm (16 in)	+	3	×	10 cm (4 in)	+	2	×	30 cm (12 in)

KING-SIZE BED QUILT (16 Squares)

QUILT SIZE*	No. of squares	×	Size of squares	+	No. of sashings	×	Width of sashings	+	No. of borders	×	Width of borders
Width 260 cm (101½ in)	4	×	45 cm (17½ in)	+	3	×	10 cm (4 in)	+	2	×	25 cm (9¾ in)
Length 260 cm (101½ in)	4	×	45 cm (17½ in)	+	3	×	10 cm (4 in)	+	2	×	25 cm (9¾ in)

QUILTS WITHOUT SASHING

SINGLE-BED QUILT (15 Squares)

	No. of squares	×	Size of squares	+		×		+	No. of borders	×	Width of borders
Width 165 cm (65¼ in)	3	×	35 cm (13¾ in)					+	2	×	30 cm (12 in)
Length 235 cm (93¾ in)	5	×	35 cm (13¾ in)					+	2	×	30 cm (12 in)
Width 170 cm (67½ in)	3	×	40 cm (16 in)					+	2	×	25 cm (9¾ in)
Length 250 cm (99½ in)	5	×	40 cm (16 in)					+	2	×	25 cm (9¾ in)

DOUBLE-BED QUILT (12 Squares)

	No. of squares	×	Size of squares	+		×		+	No. of borders	×	Width of borders
Width 204 cm (81 in)	3	×	48 cm (19 in)					+	2	×	30 cm (12 in)
Length 252 cm (100 in)	4	×	48 cm (19 in)					+	2	×	30 cm (12 in)
Width 200 cm (78 in)	3	×	50 cm (19½ in)					+	2	×	25 cm (9¾ in)
Length 250 cm (97½ in)	4	×	50 cm (19½ in)					+	2	×	25 cm (9¾ in)

QUEEN-SIZE BED QUILT (20 Squares)

	No. of squares	×	Size of squares	+		×		+	No. of borders	×	Width of borders
Width 220 cm (86 in)	4	×	40 cm (15½ in)					+	2	×	30 cm (12 in)
Length 260 cm (101½ in)	5	×	40 cm (15½ in)					+	2	×	30 cm (12 in)
Width 220 cm (86 in)	4	×	45 cm (17½ in)					+	2	×	20 cm (8 in)
Length 265 cm (103½ in)	5	×	45 cm (17½ in)					+	2	×	20 cm (8 in)

KING-SIZE BED QUILT (16 Squares)

	No. of squares	×	Size of squares	+		×		+	No. of borders	×	Width of borders
Width 260 cm (102 in)	4	×	50 cm (19½ in)					+	2	×	30 cm (12 in)
Length 260 cm (102 in)	4	×	50 cm (19½ in)					+	2	×	30 cm (12 in)

*Imperial measurements have been adjusted or rounded up or down as appropriate to help the reader

TELEPHONE BOOK COVER

This would not only make a very practical gift but also an attractive addition to any telephone table. Choose a fabric that launders well. As telephone directories tend to differ in size, measure the book for your area and adjust the measurements accordingly.

Materials
31 cm x 68 cm (12¼ in x 26½ in) calico or desired plain fabric
31 cm x 68 cm (12¼ in x 26½ in) thin polyester wadding/batting
31 cm x 68 cm (12¼ in x 26½ in) fabric for lining

1. Draw a line vertically 21.5 cm (8⅜ in) from the raw edge on the right-hand side of the fabric to be candlewicked and another horizontally 15.5 cm (6¼ in) from the top raw edge (fig 1).

2. Match the centre lines of the fabric with those of the design and trace the design onto the fabric.

3. Place the fabric in the hoop and pull taut. Candlewick the design and when the candlewicking is complete, wash and iron the fabric carefully, following the instructions on page 8.

4. Tack the wadding/batting to the lining around the edges. Turn under a 5 mm (¼ in) seam allowance along one short side of both the candlewicked fabric and the lining. Press.

5. With right sides together, pin and tack the front to the lining along the other three sides. Machine stitch using an overlock stitch or a straight and then a zigzag stitch. Clip the corners and turn right side out. Slipstitch the open end closed.

6. Prepare for quilting and quilt the design (and the rest of the fabric, if desired) as described on page 12.

7. Turn the rectangle of quilted fabric over (with the lining uppermost) and fold over 9 cm (3½ in) towards the lining at both ends as shown. Stitch close to the top and bottom edges of the pockets (fig 2). Remove the tacking threads.

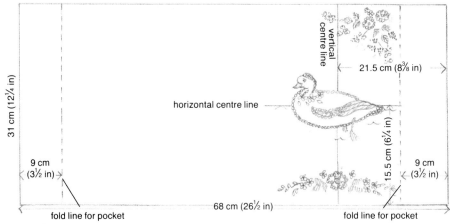

Fig 1

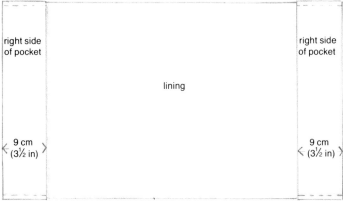

Fig 2

TABLECLOTH

Materials for a square cloth
71 cm x 71 cm (28 in x 28 in) calico or
other fabric of desired colour
3 m x 3-7 cm-wide (3¼ yds x 1¼-2¾ in-
wide) lace

1. Matching the raw edges of the corner
of the fabric with those of the design on
page 82, trace the designs onto one or
more corners.

2. Place the corners, one at a time, in the
hoop and pull taut. Candlewick all the
designs, finishing off the back of the
work very neatly.

3. Once all the candlewicking is
complete, wash and iron the fabric well,
following the instructions on page 8.

4. Make a hem along the top and bottom
edges first and then along the two side
edges by turning under 5 mm (¼ in) and
then 1 cm (½ in). Pin, tack and machine
stitch. Alternatively the corners can be
mitred as shown.

5. Sew the lace to the right side of the
tablecloth as near to the edge as
possible, mitring the corners.

> **To calculate the fabric required for a
> tablecloth.**
> Measure the length and breadth of the
> table and add on 10 cm (4 in) all round.
> For example, if a table measures 50 cm
> (20 in) square, you will need a piece of
> fabric 60 cm (24 in) square.

TABLE NAPKINS

Choose a cotton or any other fabric that
has enough body to stay crisp and fresh-
looking when laundered.

Materials
For a set of six
114 cm x 76 cm (1 ¼ yds x 30 in) fabric
10 m x 3 cm-wide (11 yds x 1 ¼ in-wide)
lace (optional)

1. Cut the fabric into six 38 cm x 38 cm
(15 in x 15 in) pieces.

2. Trace the design onto one or more
corners of each square, matching the
corner of the design with those of the
napkin.

3. Place them one at a time in the hoop
and pull taut. Candlewick the designs
and then wash and iron the pieces of
fabric, following the instructions on
page 8.

4. Make a hem around all four sides of
each napkin by turning over 5 mm
(¼ in) and then another 5 mm (¼ in),
mitring the corners.

5. If you like lacy linen, pin, tack and
machine stitch the lace to the edge of
each napkin, mitring the corners.

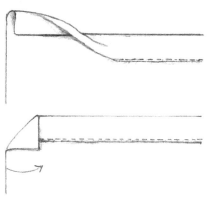
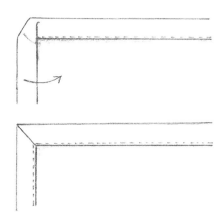

Mitring corners on a hem

Mitring corners in lace

CUSHIONS

There is nothing more inviting than a comfortable chair, sofa or bed with lots of plump, pretty cushions on it. Add a cup of tea and a book and you'll be all set for a delightful afternoon!

Cushions are really very easy to make once you know how. Whether they are ruffled or plain, elegant cushions, they must be completely washable and practical, so choose fabrics and lace that launder well. Remember to wash enough fabric for the cushion front, back and ruffle.

Bear in mind that the cushion will become much smaller once it is stuffed.

Materials for a plain square cushion
47 cm x 47 cm (18½ in x 18½ in) fabric for front
47 cm x 47 cm (18½ in x 18½ in) polyester wadding/batting
47 cm x 47 cm (18½ in x 18½ in) muslin
50 cm (19½ in) zip
47 cm x 49 cm-wide (18½ in x 19¼ in-wide) fabric for back

1. Fold the fabric for the front in half horizontally and then vertically and finger-press.

2. Match the centre lines of the fabric with those of your design and trace the design onto the fabric.

3. Place in a hoop and pull taut. Candlewick the design and when complete, wash and iron the fabric very carefully, following the instructions on page 8.

4. Sandwich the wadding/batting between the cushion front and the muslin (or old, plain sheeting) and tack from the centre to the edges and then from the centre to the corners.

5. Quilt the fabric as described on page 12.

6. Fold the fabric for the back of the cushion in half vertically and finger-press. Cut along the fold line.

7. Turn under 1 cm (½ in) to the wrong side along one long side of each half and finger-press. Place the zip, right side up, between the two pieces of fabric. Tack and machine stitch using a zipper foot. Remove tacking threads.

8. Open the zip and, with right sides facing, pin and tack the front to the back of the cushion.

9. Machine stitch around the four sides of the cushion using an overlock stitch or a straight and then a zigzag stitch. Clip the corners, remove tacking threads and turn the cushion right side out. Remove the tacking threads made in preparation for the quilting.

Materials for lace and beribboned cushion with lace ruffle
42 cm x 42 cm (16½ in x 16½ in) calico for the front
Four 44 cm (17¼ in) lengths of narrow scalloped lace
Four 44 cm (17¼ in) lengths of satin ribbon
4.25 m (4½ yds) wide cotton lace
42 cm x 42 cm (16½ in x 16½ in) polyester wadding/batting (optional)
42 cm x 42 cm (16½ in x 16½ in) prewashed muslin (optional)
44 cm x 42 cm (17¼ in x 16½ in) calico for the back

1. Fold the fabric for the front of the cushion vertically and horizontally to find the centre lines. Finger-press.

RUFFLES If you are going to make several cushions with ruffles, cut 4.5-5 m (4⅞-5½ yds) of fabric into 10-12 cm-wide (4-5 in-wide) strips. Use a narrow hemming foot, which is available for every type of sewing machine, to sew a neat hem. If using this foot, remember to move the needle slightly to the right so that it does not slip off the edge of the hem.

If you are going to make lots of ruffled items, for instance curtains, cushions, tablecloths and so on, it would be a good idea to buy a special gathering foot called a ruffler. This wonderful gadget will gather metres and metres of frill in a matter of minutes. It is important, however, to have this foot demonstrated to you first.

Double-sided ruffles If you wish to make a double-sided ruffle, cut 20-24 cm-wide (8-9½ in-wide) strips. With wrong sides facing, fold the strips in half lengthways, pin and sew. You will now have a double-sided 10-12 cm (4-5 in) ruffle.
To gather a ruffle, set the machine onto the longest stitch and sew two rows of stitching near the raw edge. Remember that a ruffle around the edge will make the cushion look much bigger.

REMOVABLE COVERS Allow at least 2 cm (⅞ in) extra across the width of the fabric for the back of your cushion if you are using a zip. For an opening like a pillow sham, allow an extra 18-20 cm (7-8 in) for the sections to overlap.

TO MAKE A SEPARATE INSIDE CUSHION, measure the cushion cover and add on 1 cm (½ in) all round. For example, if the cushion cover is 47 cm x 47 cm (18½ in x 18½ in), the inside cushion will be 49 cm x 49 cm (19¼ in x 19¼ in). Remember that the inside cushion becomes smaller once it is stuffed. Pin the two pieces of calico together. Machine stitch with an overlock stitch or a straight and then a zigzag stitch around three sides. Turn right side out and press. Stuff the cushion with polyester stuffing, pushing it right into the corners. Pin and tack the opening closed. Machine stitch using an overlock stitch or a straight and then a zigzag stitch. Trim away any ragged threads. Place the cushion inside the cover.

2. Match the centre lines of the front with those of the design and trace the design onto the fabric. The design should be no larger than 25 cm (9¾ in) square.

3. Place the fabric in a hoop and stretch taut. Candlewick the design and when complete, wash and iron the fabric carefully, following the instructions on page 8.

4. Place the candlewicked square on a flat surface. Measure and mark a line 5 cm (2 in) from the raw edge of each of the four sides.

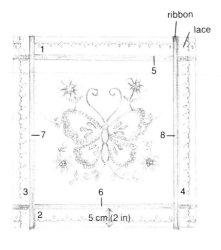

5. With the scalloped edge of the lace facing outwards, place the straight edge of one length of lace along one of the marked lines, leaving 1 cm (½ in) at each end. Pin, tack and machine stitch close to the straight edge of the lace.

6. Repeat with the remaining three lengths of lace, pinning, tacking and machine stitching them in the sequence shown in the illustration.

7. Pin one length of satin ribbon along the straight side of the first piece of lace so that the edge of the ribbon overlaps the lace and hides the stitching. Tack, then slowly machine stitch with a straight stitch along both edges of the ribbon. Repeat with the remaining ribbons as shown.

8. If you wish to quilt the design on the front, prepare the front for quilting and quilt as described on page 12.

9. Gather the cotton lace and pin it, right sides and raw edges together, to the cushion front. Leave 3 cm (1¼ in) of gathered lace loose at either end. Machine stitch the lace to the cushion front, remembering to leave the needle in the fabric and lift the presser foot about 2-3 cm (⅞-1¼ in) from the corners. Push as much lace as possible under the foot, then release the presser foot and stitch to within 6 mm (¼ in) of the corner. Once again leave the needle in the fabric and lift the presser foot. Turn the fabric and push as much lace as possible under the foot. Release the presser foot and continue stitching. Repeat the process at each corner.

10. When you reach the place where you began, sew a French seam on the raw ends of the lace as follows: With wrong sides facing, pin and machine stitch a 5 mm (¼ in) seam. Turn the seam the other way out so that right sides are facing and machine stitch a slightly wider seam than the first one. Machine stitch the lace to the fabric.

11. Complete the cushion by following the instructions on how to make a plain cushion (steps 6-10).

LAMPSHADE

All the measurements given below are for a lampshade cover that fits a 36 cm (14 in)-diameter Tiffany frame.

Materials
36 cm (14 in)-diameter Tiffany
    lampshade frame
72 cm x 72 cm (28½ in x 28½ in) calico
    or fabric of desired colour
3 m x 7 cm-wide (3¼ yds x 2¾ in-wide)
    cotton or acrylic lace
Four 75 cm x 2.5 cm-wide (29½ in x 1 in-
    wide) satin ribbons

1. Follow the instructions for making the tablecloth on page 60 steps 1-5, including the candlewicking and sewing on the lace. Finish off the embroidery on the wrong side of the cloth very neatly as it will be highlighted once it is placed on the lampshade frame and the light is switched on.

2. Find the centre point of the cloth by folding it in half horizontally and then vertically. Finger-press.

3. Measure the diameter of the top circle of the lampshade frame. Using a compass and placing it on the centre point where the horizontal and vertical lines meet, draw a circle with this diameter.

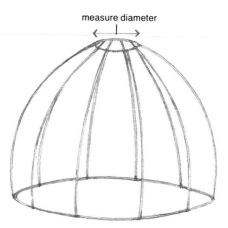

4. Using buttonhole stitch or a machine satin stitch, sew along the outline of the circle.

5. Carefully cut out the fabric within the circle.

6. Tie the satin ribbons into four bows and sew each one to the cloth, positioning them 8 cm (3¼ in) from the edge and 34.5 cm (13½ in) from each corner.

7. Place the lampshade cover over the frame and pass the light fitting (without the bulb) through the central opening. Replace the light bulb.

Quilt and bathmat design

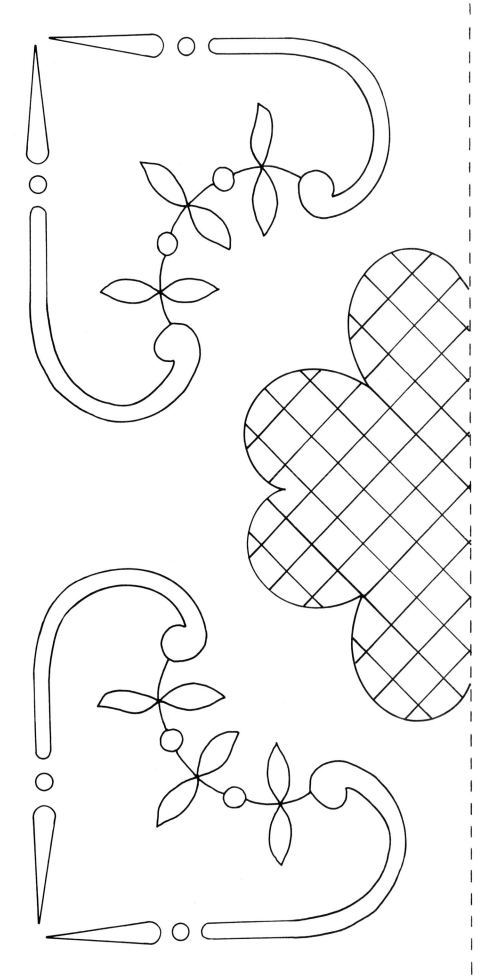

NOTE: In order to fit in as many designs as possible, it has been necessary in some cases to reproduce only half the design. Trace the design onto the tracing paper, tracing first one half and then the other to complete the design.

Apron, tea cosy, tray cloth and large tablecloth design

Tie-back quilting design

Curtain design

(Corner design suitable for tea cosy,
tablecloth, napkins, lampshade etc)

Sheet design

Quilt and cushion design

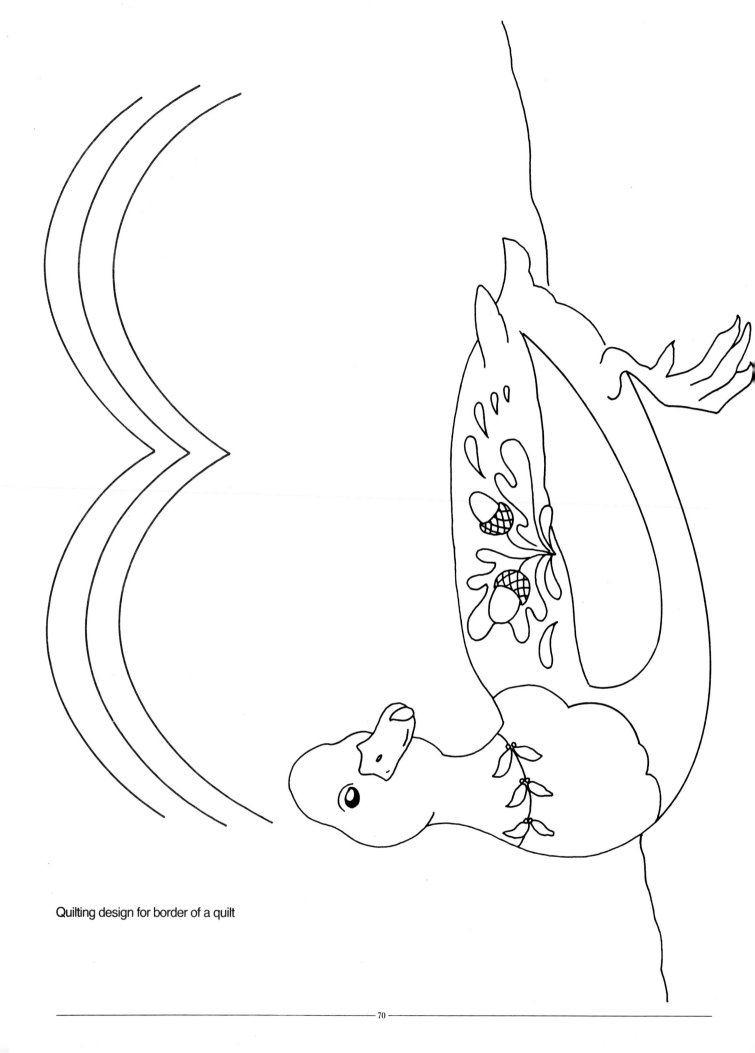

Quilting design for border of a quilt

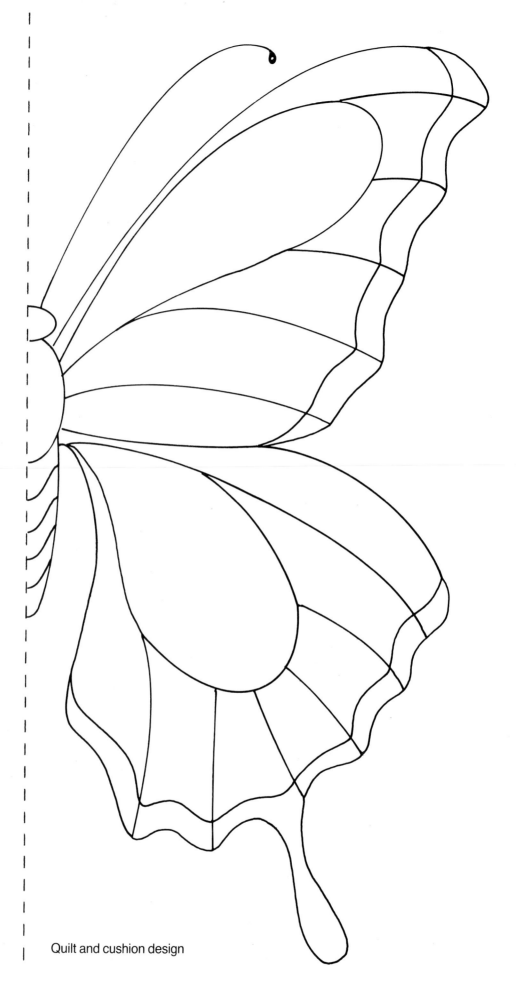

Quilt and cushion design

Quilt and cushion design

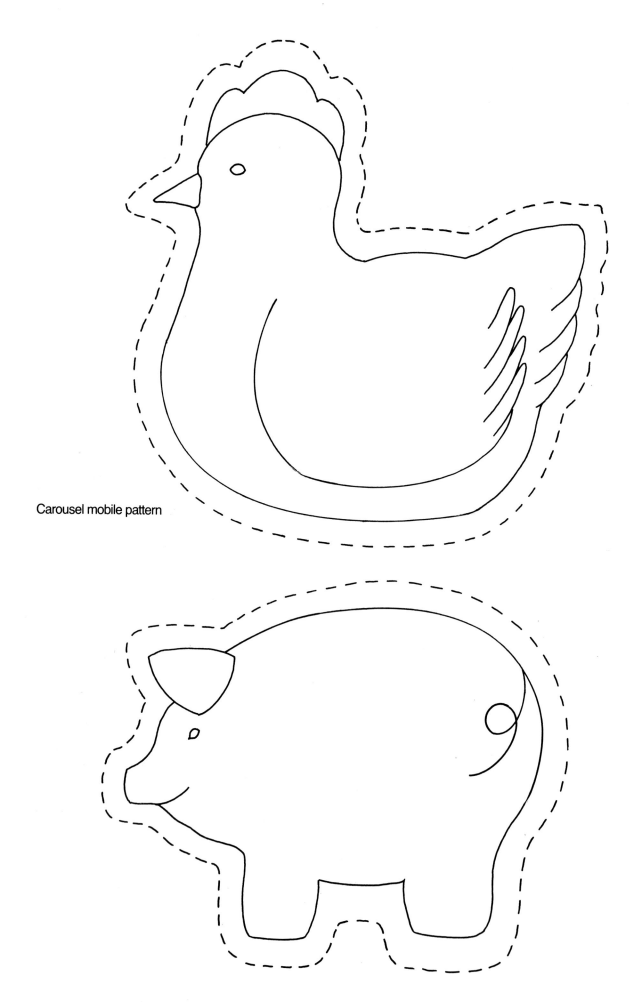

Carousel mobile pattern

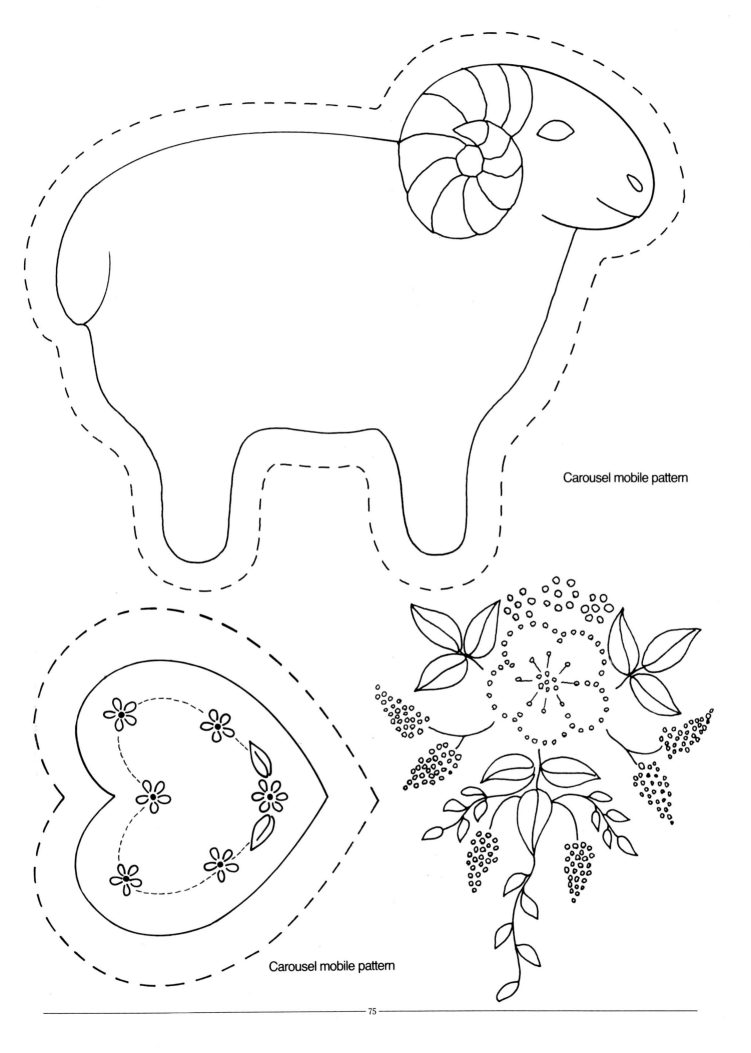

Carousel mobile pattern

Carousel mobile pattern

Tea cosy pattern and design

Place on fold

Pillowcase design

Quilt and cushion design

Quilt and cushion design

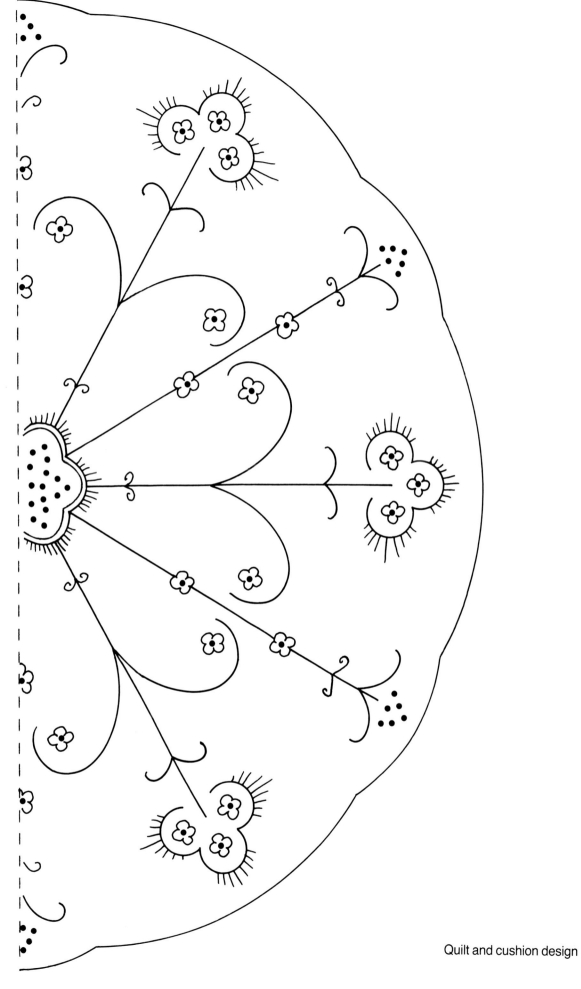

Quilt and cushion design

ribbon position

Tissue box holder pattern

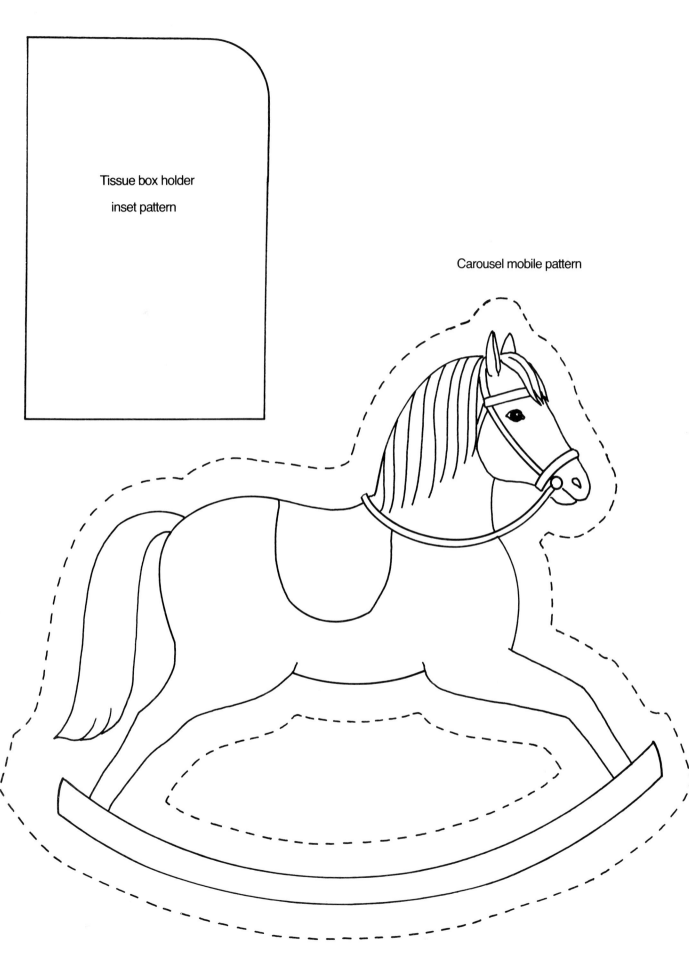

Tissue box holder

inset pattern

Carousel mobile pattern

ribbon position

Apron bib pattern

Quilt and cushion design

Quilt and cushion design

Quilt and cushion design

Quilt and cushion design

Quilt and cushion design

Quilt and cushion design

Guest towel design

Oven gloves pattern

Oven gloves pocket pattern and design

Cot quilt design

Cot quilt design

INDEX

Candlewick/quilting hoops and
additional sets of designs are
available from:
Willowtree Products cc,
P O Box 103, Somerset West 7130.
Tel: (024) 24914.